QUICK SHOTS OF FALSE HOPE

a rejection collection

SPIKE

AN AVON BOOK

AVON BOOKS, INC.
1350 Avenue of the Americas
New York, New York 10019

Copyright © 1999 by Laura Kightlinger
Interior design by Kellan Peck
Published by arrangement with the author
ISBN: 0-380-81046-8
www.spikebooks.com

Library of Congress Cataloging in Publication Data:
Kightlinger, Laura.
Quick shots of false hope : a rejection collection /
Laura Kightlinger.
p.   cm.
"An Avon book."
1. Rejection (Psychology) Humor.   I. Title.
PN6231.R39K56   1999   99-27581
818'.5408—dc21   CIP

First Spike Printing: October 1999

SPIKE TRADEMARK REG. U.S. PAT. OFF. AND IN OTHER COUNTRIES,
MARCA REGISTRADA, HECHO EN U.S.A.

Printed in the U.S.A.

OPM   10   9   8   7   6   5   4   3   2   1

In ongoing memory of

Arilda Loli and Joseph Patrick Murphy

acknowledgments

With love and gratitude to my writer adviser friends

   Nancy Shayne

     Alison Pollet

       Lee Buttala

without whom I'd still be reading these stories to myself in the mirror.

And king-sized thanks to my friend Linda Paulls, who said, "When you leave out the disgusting details, you're cheating the reader."

And to my mom, who said, "Why are you so morbid—is it because of me?"

And to my editor, Tom Dupree, a man who waited for me to finish.

A heartfelt, if awkward, high-five to my literary agent, Jack Horner, for continuing to praise me to others long after he actually believed it.

contents

Jimmy Archer

99

Big

85

The Customer's
Always Right

105

Strawberry
Swirl

115

Building
Dorothy

123

You
Always
Hurt

139

QUICK
SHOTS OF
FALSE
HOPE

Carwash

I was determined to show my high school a side of me they didn't know or care existed. A side that demanded praise no matter who got hurt. Having already made forays into the dramatic arts playing a therapist in *David and Lisa* and the mother in *You Can't Take It with You*, I was now ready to assume my rightful place. Not just as Forrester High's best actor, but as its star.

At first glance, the chunk of my life that I spent beating a path to that high-school stage was pathetic; but in retrospect it was just the beginning. It was when I started asking for outside assistance—my "Please, please God" phase. Everything meant so much. "Please, please God, let me be in the high-school play. Please, please God, I won't ask for another thing if I can be in the fall musical or be the president of Drama Club." As luck had it, I did end up being the president of Drama Club. But I hadn't needed to beg God. Not many kids wanted to be in the plays, and certainly no one else wanted to be president of Drama Club.

Mrs. Stanley, drama teacher and woman among men, was the only person who ever got my solid-gold, undivided attention. When she spoke, the other channels that provided me with continuous, up-to-the-minute coverage of my unpopularity, bad skin, and flat chest interrupted their broadcast to give Mrs. Stanley total access.

Of the eight students who regularly attended Mrs. Stanley's after-school Drama Club, two had lisps. One would-be-thespian was so shy that she could only lift her gaze as far as your shins when she said, "Hello." Then there was the boy who recently transferred from another school. He was too good-looking and too sought after by the cheerleading element to stay in Drama Club for long. Until he wised up, however, he had his pick of any role in any play.

Then there was Courtney Morgan, an ambitious monster in Grace Kelly clothing. She was a senior whose graduation was eagerly anticipated by everyone in the club. She had shiny-blond, pin-straight hair; clear skin; long, even, white teeth; and big breasts. She wore matching sweater sets and tight skirts and whatever type of shoe that girls whose parents "summered" at Chautauqua wore. She once asked me where I spent my summers, and I said, "Outside." She laughed so hard, a blue vein at her temple nearly broke through her translucent skin.

2 quick shots of false hope

Of course, Courtney had her pick of roles. She was planning on becoming a stage actress, so she'd wait until we left to monopolize Mrs. Stanley's time with topics like community vs. regional theater and what colleges to attend. When it was time to decide what the fall play should be, Courtney always spoke first.

"Anne," she'd start out, addressing Mrs. Stanley by her first name, "we need to break out of the babyish, high-school play rut. I want to do a classic, but I don't see any point in going down the O'Neill road again. What if we put up *St. Joan?*"

I instantly started to think of what *I* could play in *St. Joan.* I couldn't think of anything. "Well," I proposed matter-of-factly, "since there probably aren't many parts for women in that play, and so many women audition, why don't we just have Courtney do a monologue to kind of introduce the fall play, and then have an actual play that the rest of us could participate in?"

Marlene, one of the lispers, snickered and then covered her mouth with her fingertips. Darren, the other lisper, who was blond and effeminate and loved me unconditionally, agreed, "That's not a bad idea."

"It's a horrible idea, you little fool!" Courtney snapped.

Mrs. Stanley smiled and said something utterly diplomatic like, "Well, that's why we need this club. We have to discuss everything until the perfect solution presents itself."

Courtney glowered at me. I felt like I'd won something.

Since Courtney would be graduating, a quarter of the club lisped, and the other eighth was too good-looking to continue on with the untouchables, I was starting to look invaluable—at least in my estimation.

Darren came up to me in the school parking lot after the meeting and thrust his palm out in front of my face in a high five. I slapped it. "That was fucking great! Do you know how many times I've wanted to say something to that selfish bitch?" he lisped. "And you did it!" He put his hand out again, and I slapped it a second time and laughed, reliving the victory. "And you said it in front of the whole class and in such a cool way that it was just . . . *ohhh*"—he raised his fists over his head like he was crossing an imaginary finish line—"perfect!" And then he hugged me. I stiffened up like a cartoon character struck by an arrow. Darren had a crush on me, and he sometimes got a little too tactile. In fact, he took any and every opportunity to get too close to me physically. Which ultimately made me hate us both.

"Oh," he said, backing away from me, "I forgot you don't like to be touched."

"No, it's not that—I, just, um, ya know, I wasn't expecting you to do that just then," I said, in a verbal doggy paddle toward nothing. He knew I didn't like to be touched by him, and I'd lied about it so much that all of a sudden it was my God-given quirk: I was the girl who didn't like to be touched. I didn't mind if that was something people thought about me because the type of guy that would've touched me in high school was a type that I most definitely didn't want to be touched by.

The foundation of our friendship wasn't very strong. It was built on Darren's shameless worship of me and my need of shameless worship. I wasn't getting any other male attention—although I tried as much as anyone could. I was deeply involved in extracurricular activities in high school, like setting up the concession stand before the football games. I wore jeans so tight, nothing was left to the imagination except how I got into them. Still, I never got anything from the football players.

That didn't stop my deluded fantasies. I was electrifying myself with anticipation, force-feeding a letdown: setting up cups, putting out bags of M&Ms, making myself look useful and team spirited though I was only thinking about some vague one-on-one with a jock. I tried to get close to the football players when I handed them a soda or gave them change; I wanted my invasion into their personal space to seem like an accident—like I'd lost my balance or slipped on some Pepsi—but each "slipup" was premeditated. I wanted to get next to their sweaty bodies. To me, the scent of sweat and mud and grass was what you smelled on the doorstep of "it": sex. And if you were lucky, someone would open that door and for five luxurious minutes, grind everything they had (and even what they didn't) into your person.

One day after school I helped Mrs. Stanley hang posters urging students to audition for the gong show organized by the senior class to raise money for their trip to Florida.

My cousin Jay was going to be one of the judges. He was a star basketball player who didn't know that I existed except for the times when he saw me at the kitchen table at his house when my aunt Ardeen invited me and my mother to have dinner with her family. "C'mon over, I got plenty," she'd say. The truth was, she cooked too much on purpose. My mom and I often dropped by to eat—not because we were freeloaders but because my mom didn't have time to cook. She was a telephone operator so her shifts were always changing. And she usually did extra shifts—sometimes twelve hours at a time—because we needed the money.

On one such occasion when my mom and I were at my aunt's house eating, Jay came home drenched in sweat from basketball practice. My mom told him that Jody and I were preparing something for the gong show.

"Good," he cracked, gulping a glass of milk and wiping his mouth with his shirt, "somebody's got to get gonged."

Jody was my best friend. We'd met on the playground in the second grade and had been friends ever since. She had gleamy blue eyes and a small pointy nose that I constantly reminded her was the kind of genetic good luck that most people would kill for. Her hair was blond and only existed to be fried with a curling iron every morning. Our town didn't

quick shots of false hope

offer much in the way of new and original hairstyles. It seemed like the rest of the world was enjoying the future with its modern eighties hairstyles, but someone or something kept our town feathered back like Farrah Fawcett.

Jody's body was shapely but not the shape she wanted, and she slumped into it accordingly. We both maintained just about the worst posture of any girls in our high school.

I noticed it one day. "We're turtles," I told Jody.

"What do you mean?" she asked.

"Well, our backs are curved, and we walk with our faces down," I explained.

"That's because no one looks at us anyway," she answered.

That statement really stung.

"That's not true!" I countered, feeling the need to defend our worth.

"Well, no one looks at *me*," she said.

"OK, now, that's bullshit," I said. "Just because no one looks at us here in this school doesn't mean we're not good-looking. What about when we were at the Erie County Gala Days? Everybody looked at us there."

"Everybody there was drunk and about fifty years old."

"OK, we're dogs—is that what you want me to say?" I asked, deflated. "Wait a minute," I then went on. "I just remembered a *forty*-year-old that looks at you," I said, wishing I hadn't.

carwash 7

"Yuck, that's true," she said. "Only he just looks at my chest."

"Eww, that pig."

Jody's breasts were big, and they brought the kind of attention she didn't want and that I took personally. I could remember everything about the moment that we both caught Mr. Stenquist getting an eyeful. Jody and I were taking a science test in Mr. Stenquist's class, and he was walking around to make sure no one was cheating. Jody was wearing a black sweater with three white penguins on it. Looking over her shoulder, allegedly to see how she was doing on her paper, that smooth-operator-turned-pedantic-natural-science-bore slurped, "I like your penguins, Jody." It really made me ill. When anyone is leering, especially a man and specifically a man leering at my friend's breasts, it renders me . . . genderless. I feel like an inanimate object. Mr. Stenquist's unsolicited cheap thrill, at my best friend's expense, turned me into a telephone pole.

Jody possessed this kind of corn-fed innocence that seemed to elicit unsavory male response. She was beautiful in a hearty, open, sympathetic way that couldn't filter out the scum. I once stayed overnight at her house, and her father, who was an amenable, overweight, part-owner of a Mace Electronics store, was sitting in the living room with a friend of his who worked for Falconer Plate & Glass. Jody and I walked through the room in our nightgowns to get a late-night snack and take it back upstairs with us. As we walked through the living room, her dad commented to his friend: "Well, looks like Jody's developing." I thought, "My God! Her father just objectified her, and both of them are looking at us in our nightgowns!" And *I* wasn't even mentioned.

We both tried to transfer out of Mr. Stenquist's class after the "penguin incident," but we were halfway through the course and would lose the credit if we left.

Jody and I planned our schedules around each other. We were together in all but one class: She took German, and I took Spanish. We thought we'd do the bare minimum needed to graduate and then concentrate on our performing careers. But when I told her about the gong show, she wasn't as excited as someone who wanted to perform. She had this paranoid notion that not having any discernible talent might hurt us in a situation where people were supposed to show off their talent. I begged to differ and sold her a bill of goods, that it was her nature to believe. So began the intense rehearsals held outside, where I "summered."

We moved my stereo to the back porch, pressed the speakers against the screen door, and went to work choreographing a combination dance and gymnastics routine to one of 1978's most popular songs, "Carwash." Since Jody and I were gifted, I figured that we'd probably get more attention from our performance than we could even fathom. As I saw it, we'd be discovered and asked to appear on a televised talent show. Or better. Because I had this vague notion of "the high-school spotlight," I'd imagined that we'd not only be invited back to do a repeat performance at the high school, but eventually we would be bused to the nearest entertainment capital—Buffalo, of course—where we would do a few live performances. Soon after, Carol Burnett would get wind of us. Or Merv Griffin. Or both. Then everyone would have posters of us in their bedrooms. We'd be posing in the best platforms that money could buy with a caption running alongside our sleek torsos that read: TOO COOL FOR HIGH SCHOOL! WE'RE FUNKTASTIC!

At the moment that we realized "our act" was too hot to be confined to a backyard, the big day was upon us. We were bristling with show-day excitement when we met for a full-dress rehearsal, complimenting ourselves on everything right down to the toes of our striped toe socks. Over wings and bleu cheese we made a pact to kick ass. I remember waiting behind the red-velvet curtains on the auditorium stage, bouncing with my hands on my knees like I'd seen the dancers do on *Soul Train*. I was so nervous and revved up that I was hyperventilating. I tried to stop by taking deep breaths and shaking out my hands and feet as if it were something one did before a gong show. Jody was on the other side of the stage, snapping her fingers and focusing. I thought she looked surprisingly professional doing that, and when I caught her eye, I smiled and pulled my fists in at my waist with a

quick shots of false hope

quick jerk. It was a gesture of solidarity that I'd seen the cheerleaders use. It meant: "Let's go out there and fuck 'em up." Jody sent the signal back to me.

The high-school auditorium stage was empty except for our one prop, a car we had fashioned out of cardboard and painted yellow and black. I don't know why we didn't realize it at the time, but the car looked too small and one dimensional to resemble anything real, let alone a life-sized car that real teenagers were about to wash. Then again, we also ignored the fact that our other props—two hoses that weren't connected to anything and some rags—didn't make much sense, either.

The curtain rose, and there we were: Jody, holding a rag, and me with a hose, wiggling our asses, our backs to the audience. At that moment, as the music swelled and the hot light bore down on my rear end, I had the first inkling that maybe this wasn't such a good idea. I was so bent on railroading Jody into this ridiculous scheme, I'd inadvertently convinced myself that it was a standout concept. The fact that I didn't allow myself to stroll down any avenue of possible disaster prior to this moment was masochistic. I felt myself burning inside from doubt, from the knowledge that the audience was going to turn on us—if they hadn't already. Once again, with my mouth to God's deaf ear, I pleaded: "Please let us finish without getting gonged."

I was going through my moves in a manic, over-inflated

way, making eye contact with Jody and trying to keep my spirits up. When the words "Hey, get your car wash today" came up full, we turned and faced the huge auditorium audience. We dropped our "washing gear" and cartwheeled in front of the car. Then Jody did a backflip. Since I couldn't do one of those, I clasped my hands and stepped through the circle made by my outstretched arms, a move I'd seen "The Lockers"—this black dance group—do on a variety show. Some of the audience was clapping to the beat, but I was losing faith in our presentation while we were presenting it. "This would seem cool if we were doing this at a party," I told myself. "At someone's party we'd seem like hot-shit dancers." But we were in front of about three hundred people who had bought tickets.

At some point we did the bump, but I was wishing we could do something different, something mesmerizing, to make it seem like we weren't two teenagers shaking our money makers at a party. I was trying to think fast, wondering if I could improvise something that wouldn't throw Jody off—but the two of us were just too basic. My only resort was to make it look like outrageous fun, which was difficult since the song was lasting an eternity, like maybe it was skipping or maybe they'd played it twice to toy with us.

Finally our last manuever, which really was quite difficult (for us), was set in motion. I did a handstand, and Jody did a handstand a few feet away from me. As planned, I came

quick shots of false hope

down from my handstand in a "crab position," and with my stomach high in the air, Jody was to do a front flip over my extended frame. I didn't realize I was too close to the stage lights, so Jody had no room to do her flip unless she wanted to fly off the stage into the front-row seats. Rather than stand still, she danced and clapped to the beat. I was feeling my elbows shake and thinking, *"What the hell is she doing?!"* Then she stood back and did a front hand-spring as my arms gave out and I fell on my back.

At which point we were gonged.

For some reason I couldn't get up right away. I was on my back on an auditorium stage in front of the entire junior and high schools, and I needed to lie there and mull it over in my mind for a few extra seconds. Jody came over and offered her hand. Looking up at her pink sweat-streaked face and apologetic smile made me think, for a second, that it was all her fault. She'd botched what should have been our signature finale by leaving me hanging out there while she messed around with some amateurish tumble. I grabbed Jody's hand, and she pulled me up. The emcee waved us over. The distance to the side of the stage, where the emcee had walked on as we were gonged, seemed like a walk across a playing field. Jody started to whisper an explanation as to how the whole thing went south. I was giving her my ear without listening; scrambling for the miracle excuse, impromptu line, anything to save our collective asses. The only way to make a clean break of it was to go up to the emcee, grab his microphone with confidence, and say the funniest thing ever. I had to make it seem like the whole thing had been a joke, that Jody and I couldn't possibly have been so moronic as to have created and rehearsed something as stupid as a dance with a garden hose and a cardboard car.

But I didn't get my chance. The emcee, a popular upperclassman and one of the funniest guys that I vaguely knew in high school, took Jody's hand and my hand and stood between us. He handed us each a root-beer barrel, saying, "Here, one for you and one for you because we liked your moves. Lay-dees!" He gibed, licking his lips and gyrating his pelvis. The crowd howled their approval, and I smiled to keep my face from giving way to sadness, I was still reaching for the funny quip that would absolve us and show the audience it was all in good fun. But even if the clever something was there, I couldn't use it, because I didn't know if it would come out before the tears that I'd been holding in since the wand hit the gong (or the shit hit the fan).

The fact that the same high-school auditorium that had embraced me as Penelope Sycamore in *You Can't Take It with You* dropped me like a hot rock when I slammed through the "Carwash" pantomime proved that the theater is a fickle bitch. So, with my ego pulverized and spirit frayed at both ends, I skulked off the stage. Jody told me what had happened, that I'd been lying too close to the stage lights for her to jump.

quick shots of false hope

She was taking this loss a lot better than I was. Then again, I don't think she ever wanted superstardom like I did.

Within seconds, I was replaying the moments leading up to our discourteous removal by the judges. I decided that one of the factors working against us, besides the cardboard washing, the beginner-level floor routine, and the fall, was that Betsy Tanning performed before us.

Betsy had won every high-school championship gymnastics competition, and all of her moves were crisp and hard and certain. To the tune of Eric Carmen's "All By Myself," Betsy did backflips and front flips and walked on her hands while scissoring her hard, fat legs and concluded with a flawless, groin-defying, sideways split. She knew her body and knew exactly what it was going to do and when it was going to do it. In stark contrast, all we knew about our bodies was that mine was underdeveloped and Jody's was overdeveloped. We couldn't trust our bodies as far as we couldn't throw them.

Funktastic we weren't. After the show I ran out to the car with my mother and informed her that I had to switch schools. We went to my grandmother's house, and the minute I got there, I ran to her bed and cried into the pillows. I did it again when I got home. So technically I cried through two houses that night. And I didn't just cry. I wailed with the kind of eighth-grade suffocating hate for my lot in life that comes out in short spurts of self-pity directed at others—in this case, my mother. "I . . . ah . . . I . . . it would be one thing if I were popular or even pretty and I had this embarrassing thing happen, but to look like me thanks to you for sleeping with my ugly dog of a dad and then have this happen and have to go to school tomorrow and face this with *my* face, ahh, and flat chest— God! Why do I live!"

I thought that it had just been the worst day of my life. I was wrong.

The next day was the worst day of my life.

It started the moment I walked into homeroom. A few of the boys mimicked washing something, waving their hands in a circular motion, parodying words from the song like: "Get your cardboard today, if you fall on your ass you can't stay. . . ." Even Michelle Westzinger, the tallest girl in the eighth grade, who had frizzy hair and braces and knew what it was to be the brunt of a joke, was laughing at me. She even took part in it, imitating me with the same expressions that the boys were using. So at my expense, for one brief moment, Michelle Westzinger had a chance to experience how the popular half lived.

Our performance must've been extra-juicy bad because it was feasted on by classmates like hyenas on a zebra carcass. They nibbled it, walked around with pieces of our hide in their mouths, lay in the sun savoring it. It seemed there was no end to the joy they reaped from it.

I saw Jody at lunch and asked her if she was getting a

quick shots of false hope

lot of shit. She said she was, but since she was even less popular than I was, she could hang out in the "loadie" corner. The loadies were the poorest kids and the poorest students at our high school. They were considered tough and unruly but were actually sweet and neglected like the characters in the 1930s Bowery Boys' movies. Another similarity: You could only see them in black and white. The loadies were given their own section of the high school so that they could smoke and unwind while being outcasts. Jody found a safe haven with the loadies because they were oblivious to the high-school loop. In fact, they would never go to a function that the rest of the high school would attend. So they didn't know or care about the debacle that was suppposed to have been our star turn.

Ponderosa

Tammy was a five-foot-one blond who had been told she was cute enough times to make it her business. Full-to-bursting in every area of her brown Ponderosa polyester dress, she was looking over the manager's shoulder at my application while he was interviewing me. She gave me a fake smile and a thumbs up before tapping him on the shoulder and interrupting the interview for something *urgent*. When he turned back to me, the fuel in my ass-kissing tank was so low I had to hitch a ride back to "barely giving a shit." He said the words "loyalty" and "commitment" so many times, I thought I was joining the army. In my head I was saying: "C'mon, you dick, it's a three-dollar-an-hour *waitressing* job!" But it came out in front of present company like: "I just really love working with people."

I must admit I was completely devastated when I saw the outfits we had to wear, but I overcame it for cash to buy beer with my friends on the weekends. And to feel a bit of independence from my mother.

Tammy wore a gold tag, which meant she'd been working at the prestigious establishment known as the Ponderosa Steakhouse for more than two years and had won the coveted title of assistant manager—which was another way of saying that she'd been predestined to be a bitch. She had it out for me in a big way from the start. I think it was because I tried to have fun. I made other people laugh while on the job. And—as I was soon to find out—in a family-style restaurant run a certain way by middle-management plebes, there are no laughs. Just a dedication to monotonous service to ensure that the all-you-can-eat days glide efficiently into the all-you-can-eat nights. If people could be fed for slaughter, this would be the place where they'd come to bulk up.

The booths were cramped, the food was cheap and bad, and all that mattered was abundance. I think one of the Ponderosa slogans was "You get more." More shit than you could possibly want or ever eat—but everyone tried. Some people ate so much that it made me feel sick to my stomach. On one of the all-you-can-eat nights I brought chicken filets to a couple who must have weighed three hundred and fifty pounds each and their two-hundred-pound kids, who were probably about seven and ten years old. Before I set down their fourth helping, I wanted to say, "Please, for the love of God, do something together besides eating! Go bowling or swimming or, Heaven forbid, take a bike ride!"

One night when I was extremely tired and feeling espe-

quick shots of false hope

cially bad because exams and the prom were coming up and I wasn't going to fare well in either situation, I heard Tammy talking in the kitchen while I was taking my fourth tray of breaded-fish patties to a table that wasn't one of my usual all-you-can-eat families. (Most of the families I got to know—sometimes by name—because of their regular appearances.) During the first three weeks that I was there, the powers that be added an extra all-you-can-eat night to each week. I started referring to the restaurant as The Gluttony House and secretly filled out suggestion cards requesting a vomitorium.

Anyway, after one of the many family-style feeds that got me feeling low, I stacked orange plastic trays in the sink, put my coat on to leave, and did whatever else I could to add minutes to my time card before punching out. Then I over-heard Tammy just inside the kitchen doors. She was telling the manager whom I'd interviewed with, Royal (known behind his back as Royal Asshole), how I was the only one who kept forgetting to clear the ketchup bottles from the tables at the end of my shift. I stopped listening because the burden of being a loser in a polyester dress was suddenly made heavier by the weight of this brownnosed nark up my craw. Not knowing exactly what I was doing, I ran back into the dining area in my high-school jacket and Ponderosa uniform and started whipping bottles from the tables. When I had all of the condiments that my arms could hold, I went back through the swinging stainless-steel doors and threw them on the table in front of Tammy and Royal. *"There are your ketchup bottles, bitch!"* I roared and promptly stormed out. I got into my Dodge Dart and drove home mad and worried at the same time. I knew what was going to happen. I'd probably get fired. Royal loved her so much, he would eat her shit.

I got home and took off my high-school jacket. I took off my greasy Ponderosa dress and threw it on the floor. My mom had a new boyfriend, so she wasn't home. I opened the refrigerator and stood in its all-forgiving light in my Little Nothings bra and Forrester Track sweatpants. I was still staring inside the fridge when the phone rang.

It was Royal. "Hell'oo, ah, is Laura there?"

"Yes," I said tentatively, "this is Laura."

"Laura this is Royal," he said.

"Hi," I replied cautiously. For a second I had forgotten what had just happened, and I was shocked that he was calling me at home. He sounded so shaken, I thought maybe somebody had called in sick or had died.

"Laura, ah, I don't think you should come back to work. I think once you use that kind of language in front of a fellow employee that it's hard to, um, work together again."

"Oh, so I'm fired?" I asked, which I believe was the virgin voyage of a phrase that I'd spend a massive portion of my lifetime using.

"Yes, but you'll still get your last week's check. You can pick it up on Wednesday. I'm sorry that it had to be this way,

quick shots of false hope

Laura, but Tammy felt pretty bad, and as you know I'd eat her shit."

Actually, I can't remember what he said after "sorry it had to be this way," but I know it was something spineless and "family style."

I hung up the phone, cried, and went to bed. I didn't feel so bad about actually losing that job, as the prospect of not going back there didn't upset me. What upset me was that it had been my first job and I'd never known anyone who had ever been fired—not to mention fired after only two months.

The next day was Saturday, and my long-awaited menstrual cycle began. At age fifteen I was finally blessed with what other girls got at twelve. I was relieved because I had talked to the school nurse and our family doctor about it when I hadn't gotten it at fourteen, and they'd both said not to worry. And, really, what could they have told me? To leave a tampon under my pillow? The school nurse had advised me that eating more would help me get it. For a second I was almost sorry that I'd gotten it because I could have gone to the Ponderosa Steakhouse and eaten all night. And had Tammy wait on me while I yelled, "Keep bringing it, bitch! I'm not leaving until one of us bleeds!"

For a long time, I'd been pretending that I had it anyway. My mom would write a note for me saying I had cramps or migraines or both so I could get out of gym. Generally on Wednesdays, as Wednesdays were volleyball days. The gym

 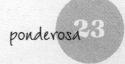

teacher picked two lady-jocks to be the captains and the rest of us sat in line on the floor and waited to be chosen. I was picked near the very end of the process which meant I found myself waiting with Meredith Wilkes and Dawn Jacobson, a skillful volleyball player except for the epileptic fits. I had the pleasure of sitting on the floor next to Dawn when she had one; her arms and legs whizzed around like a rotating sprinkler and she kicked and smacked me within an inch of my life before I could crawl away.

After my accidental beating at the hands and feet of Dawn Jacobson, I knew that my life would probably always be like this. A series of awkward moments—broken up by glints of hope. Like: at least I wasn't Meredith.

The dead last one in the high-school gym pick was Meredith Wilkes, a pale, completely isolated mess of a ninth grader. She had long, greasy, dark-blond hair and looked like she didn't belong to this century. I thought she resembled a scullery maid—and I didn't even know what that was. She had a sloppy walk, and she held her books on the way to class like a shield against cruel teenage torturers. But the books couldn't deflect the nasty remarks: "Nice pants, Meredith; did Kmart have a sale?" Her comebacks, when she felt bold enough to give one, sent her even deeper into the fresh grave of unpopularity. Her zingers typically went as follows: "No!" or "I know you are, but what am I?"—each accompanied by a snap of greasy hair and a quick about-face to avoid more shitty teenage artillery.

I felt sorry for Meredith. No one would even take a locker in her row in the girl's locker room. So I did. I said hello to her and asked her how everything was going; we small talked about tests and how much gym sucked, but we didn't form any type of bond. I think she knew I was being nice to her because she was dreadfully unpopular and I think maybe she didn't want the favor.

Meredith was standing next to her gym locker. She took off her gym shirt in a self-conscious flurry, bumping her elbow on the inside of the locker and concealing her breasts with the pink locker door. I caught a glimpse of her white polyester underwear with broken elastic hanging on her thigh, and noticed a large, dark, brownish-red splotch on the back. I looked away quickly feeling heartsick about the pain that she must be secretly dealing with. I thought about Meredith for the rest of the day. I thought about the splotch that could mean only one thing: Her ass was bleeding. "She must be really sick," I despaired. "This girl does not have an easy life." Whenever I'm feeling sorry for myself or for someone else, I have to build on it. I think of every sad thing about a situation, every indignity that a person's ever suffered, to fill out my sadness and make it a rounded, massive rock of sadness. I was thinking about Meredith's unpopularity and her less-than-great looks when I happened upon the last rusted piece of

bad news to cap the rock of sadness: Meredith's mother was the bus driver. At this moment, I had to stop my school day to step outside for a good cry. I had blasted through the rock of sadness and was left holding one gleaming gem, which I couldn't help but repeat to myself: Meredith's ass was bleeding, *and* her mother was the bus driver. "There is no God!" I told myself.

When I got home from school, I asked my mother what sort of illness would make a person's ass bleed.

"Why? Oh, God, Laura! Is your rear bleeding?" My mother's concern always sounded like blame.

"Yes, it's bleeding for your sins." I laughed at how clever I was.

"Oh, that's not funny. Is something wrong? Did you hurt yourself?!"

"No! I saw blood on the back of this girl's underwear in gym."

"Oh, Jesus, don't scare me like that! Ya know, that girl probably just got her period and wasn't prepared," my mom said matter-of-factly. I was relieved yet mortified by my own stupidity.

"Oh, yeah," I conceded, "I bet that's what it was. Do you think I'm *ever* gonna get mine?"

"Yes," she said dismissively. "Don't worry about it. When you get it, you'll wish you hadn't."

I thought that that was a typical mother thing to say.

quick shots of false hope

I'd never wished so hard for anything in my life. If I got it, I'd never wish I hadn't. I thought a menstrual cycle defined a person. I thought it would change how I felt and how I looked. I was expecting a lot of development to follow, like big breasts and all the popularity they bring. In fact, I waited until I was twenty-one for those developments—and then I forgot about it.

I never thought that on the day I'd tell my mother that all of my female organs were working, I'd also have to admit that I was no longer a working female. I had a feeling the job news would upset her, since everyone in my family kept their jobs until they got a watch.

On that particular day, my father was expected to drop by and visit, and my mom didn't feel like "seeing" him. I realized later what that meant was she didn't feel like having sex with him, which seemed to be all he came over for. He was married, and had children, so he weaseled out of family time to see us.

We lived in the same town that he lived in with his "normal" family, and this was a bit of a scandal to anyone who cared. At an early age, I was told to keep his identity a secret, which to me meant he was Batman. He'd tell his wife and kids that he was going on a business trip and meet us on the sly in fantasy locations: New York City, Miami, Puerto Rico. I thought this arrangement most beneficial. After all,

ponderosa 27

none of my friends ever went anywhere—unless the school paid for it.

My mother, on the other hand, was not so easily pleased. After more than sixteen years of illicit relations, she was bored. When she'd hear his car coming down the street but wasn't in the mood to see him, we'd shut the lights off and hide behind the couch. A lot of times it wasn't him.

At fifteen I was starting to question things that I'd never questioned before. We'd been hiding from my father on and off for over a year now. I finally said, "What the hell are we doing? Just tell him not to come over!"

"Shhh. He'll be gone in a minute."

"I'm going out to a party."

"You're just going to go out drinkin'."

"No, I'm not."

"You never want to spend any time with me. I thought we was gonna watch TV tonight."

"I can't imagine why I don't like hiding with you on a fucking Friday night."

My mom laughed.

"And by the way, I got fired yesterday."

"How come?!"

"I think it was because I was about to get my first period *ever* and I kind of lost it."

"What?!"

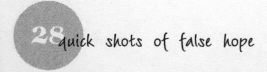
28 quick shots of false hope

"Oh, I just was sick of dealing with that bitch who hated me from the start. It was bound to happen."

"Well, you gotta try to get along with people. Do you know how many bitches I work with at the phone company every day?"

"Can we get up from here now?"

"Wait another minute."

"No! I'm going."

I felt my way along the walls of our living room and down the short hallway to the front door of our dark house, onto the porch and out to my Dodge Dart and drove to Kim Patterson's party. As I drove away, I saw my mom's head peeking out above the couch watching me leave, like a prairie dog popping out of a hole.

Internacional

I convinced my mother to let a Spanish student stay with us. I don't know why I did this. I guess I thought it would be fun.

I remember when little Christina arrived with the obligatory *Lladro*, a porcelain statuette that was the customary gift brought by Spanish students to American families in Fayetteville—and I assume across America; she opened the door to the lower-middle-class comfort of our home and was visibly disappointed. She looked a few inches to her left and then to her right like a horse freshly fitted with blinders and nodded. "Is nice." My mom graciously thanked Christina, but she could never tell when someone felt sorry for us.

I guess anyone stumbling into our house after a twenty-hour transatlantic flight would have to feel a little let down. My mom and I lived in a white two-story, two-bedroom with gold shag rug downstairs and blue shag rug upstairs. The sunken living room—which I'm sure was merely an accident, the kind of miscalculation that occurs when a family cuts corners on a spare room—was not a full step down, so most everyone tripped into it. The room was sparse: a brown couch with a burgundy maple-leaf pattern that made it feel like it was always autumn faced a large TV set in a pressed-wood console. A light-blue velvet chair that was reserved for a ghost's rear end was angled toward the TV. Actually, our *lives* were angled toward the TV. The other furniture in the house seemed to gather round the TV to listen to it, pray to it, beg it to make the days slip away.

Christina politely handed my mother the *Lladro*, a ballerina sitting cross-legged in a gray-blue tutu and matching ballerina slippers, whose face had a look of longing—presumably for some porcelain guy in Madrid.

I brought Christina up to my room at the top of the stairs. Everything matched so hard, it hurt. My bedroom carpet was yellow; the bureau and twin-sized bed were a set— with two high, white posts at the head of the bed and pink and yellow flowers painted in a line on the headboard; the walls were covered in white paneling that held yellow paint in its veins; and my bedspread was a faux-silk assault to the senses, crammed with yellow petaled black-eyed Susans. I don't know how I lived in yellow like that; it would have been the last color I would've picked to destroy—I mean, describe—my life. Oddly enough, Christina didn't like the bedroom either. I was beginning to feel like a game-show host showing a contestant an array of low-priced items on *The Price Is Right,* the last item being an above-ground pool that I hoped she might get excited about, like a housewife from Indiana. But she wasn't a housewife from Indiana; she was a goddamned brat from Spain.

It became clear that our Rice-Krispies treat welcome was the most depressing thing to happen thus far in her young life. It was as if we'd asked her to join us for a swim in a mud puddle. The lack of opulence that gushed forth changed everything she had ever heard about Americans being rich—or American families consisting of more than two women living alone.

During her stay, she spent most of her time with two other Spanish students who were visiting the Chautauqua area at the same time. The other exchange students were boys apparently in the same tax bracket as Christina's family. They looked rich and cocky, like they'd seen something of the world. For them, life was more than the pursuit of a fake ID.

While Christina was living beneath her wildest dreams at my house, she got along famously with my mother. My mom basically gave her the run of the place. One morning while my mom was at work and I was asleep, she invited her Spanish friends over to swim in the small above-ground pool in the backyard. The night before, Jody and I had invited a couple of boys over to skinny-dip and drink Strawberry Boone's Farm wine. Apparently, in my stupor, I'd ended the evening by walking into the house in a towel, leaving my underwear on the pool deck.

The next day when I woke up, I went outside to greet Christina and her guests. I was still hung over from the night before. My head felt like I'd just pulled it out of the oven, and my ears were still filled with chlorinated water. As I walked unsteadily toward the pool, I noticed that Christina had a strange look on her face. I thought she probably didn't want me to crash their Spanish clique, so I planned on saying *"ola"* and leaving. But when I got to the pool gate, I saw Christina dangling her feet over the edge and holding something at arm's length, as if she'd been forced to pick up a dead rat that had been floating around in the pool. I came closer and saw that what she was holding between her thumb and forefinger was a maxipad. One of the boys was looking down and laughing, and the other one—the one with greasy hair and teenage-minefield skin—was smiling at me.

"Oh, God!" I gulped, grabbing the pad from Christina. "Jesus, I . . . I . . ." I slobbered out regrets, but my embarrassment was swathed in venom. I couldn't even get deeply embarrassed; I was too mad at Christina for choosing to make a point of it.

She gave me a condescending half smile. She clearly wanted me to know that this was a disgrace, an international no-no that would have to be dealt with accordingly. I imagined Spanish soldiers jumping out of a helicopter and landing in the yard to make sure the life-threatening, highly explosive uranium-coated sanitary napkin was sprayed and defused while another soldier unloaded a round of shells into my person. The pad was a shock to Christina's spoiled, sheltered, five foot frame complete with matching outfits in fruit-rific colors and baby-girl polka dots. She was too delicate to bear witness to such a grisly aspect of an American girl's life—no matter that the pad was clean. I'd left it wrapped inside my underwear by the side of the pool, where it couldn't easily be mistaken for a conversation piece.

As I stood there holding my pad with my head throbbing away, I thought about saying: "When you're done out here I've left something for you in the toilet." It was incomprehensible; the thought of being straddled for a summer with this snobby little Pollyanna made my head feel hotter. It seemed to me that as a fellow female, she could have at least extended me the courtesy and sisterhoodlike gesture of telling me about it when there weren't other people around. She could have tried to hide it or dispose of it or any number of things that the AFS brochure had promised an international friend would do for you. The fusspot had pushed me too far. If I hadn't been bending over backward to make Christina's stay pleasant before this, I sure as hell was not going to lift a finger to do so now.

Luckily, my God-given gift of walking away from a problem could be put to use in dealing with Christina. I rationalized her role to be more of a Spanish daughter to my mother, thus relinquishing any responsibility that I may have had toward her. I would no longer try to show her all of the fun things that there were to do in Fayetteville—nevermind that there weren't any. She would be punished for her lack of interest in me. And I could think of no greater punishment than to let her stay in and visit with my mother while I went out to parties.

quick shots of false hope

La Ganadora

Every blunder that sprang from my best intentions seemed to facilitate a crowd. I could never have a quiet moment of personal humiliation. For some reason a witness or two had to be present to make my shame an event.

I won the Spanish poetry-reading competition that was held by area high schools at Fredonia State College by enacting a poem that I knew by heart, not by brain, called "The Olive Trees." In fact, I didn't know what the hell I was saying. I was Mr. Panna's puppet, performing by rote what he had taught me. The award, which filled my tank with confidence for about a week, brought praise from the English and Spanish Departments and granted me clemency for a public-relations fuckup that could have cost me my Spanish wings.

I believe it all started when a gorgeous Spanish exchange student named Juan and his astronomically wealthy parents came to visit our school. Mr. Panna was giving them a tour of the high school and happened across me in an art class,

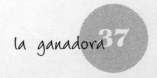

where he wanted me, on command, to tell Juan's parents, in Spanish, what I was doing at that moment. I told him, in English, that I didn't know how to say what I was doing, which was drawing.

And Mr. Panna said, "Well, conjucate a verb from what you've learned in class today."

Still drawing a blank, I said, "Juego con yo mismo," which I found out later means, "I am playing with myself."

The exchange student's parents smiled, and Mr. Panna didn't say anything; he just whisked them away from me.

Mr. Panna was known for turning simple situations into blown-out dramas. He could transform a glance into soap-opera fodder, and if someone laughed at his rendition, there would be a performance for every class for the rest of the semester. I guess you could say he liked to play everything to the hilt. A story about a trip to the supermarket could include hand waving, hip shaking, desk pounding, and every sort of unnecessary affect that you could imagine. I sometimes found myself laughing along with the class at him, even though I hated to. I felt too above it all to join in with the immature antics of this robust clown.

When I walked into his class, the Monday after the talent show debacle, it seemed as if I'd been granted clemency. And then it came. With his back turned to the class, while he was writing on the board he launched in on me:

"Laudita, I saw the talent show, and I thought you and Jody were *sooo* cute."

A few of the boys in class started to laugh.

"Shhhhh, Georgie-Porgie," he scolded.

George was a freshman with an identical twin. Both George and his twin, Henry, were pint-sized and friendly. It had been revealed during one of Mr. Panna's "playful" interrogations, that their father made them cut their hair airforce-short. Consequently, they were incessantly fiddling with it, patting it down, pushing it forward with their fingers to cover their cardoor ears.

"Georgie, I don't want any of you making fun because no one in here had the courage to get on stage like Laudita." Mr. Panna eyed the class before he moved in for the kill. He sat on the corner of his desk that was closest to me.

"And your outfits were adorable. Now, honey, was the stage slippery?" A couple of students started sniggering.

"No, I'm just a klutz," I replied.

"Hmm. Well, when I saw you go back like this—" He got up and walked to the front and center of his desk, then leaned backward with his arms flailing, prompting the twins and the rest of the class to laugh and applaud his reenactment. "Anyway, Lauda, when I saw you"—he did it a second time because he loved the spotlight—"I said, 'Oh, no, *mi amiga Lauda ha estado en un accidente grave!*'" Then he

laughed at his own dramatization. "Well, it doesn't matter, Lauda," he said. *"Tu sabe amoramos."*

I didn't say anything.

"Do you know what I said, Lauda?"

"Uh, we love you?"

"Sí, sí, es claro, Laudita." At which point he came over and hugged me in my chair.

Mr. Panna took an interest in me personally because what I lacked in aptitude, I made up for in attendance. There were days when I genuinely liked Mr. Panna and other days when his flamboyance wore on me. Once a month, he'd bring in some sort of artifact: a piece of music or an article of clothing that was native to certain cities in Spain. He would choose one of us as a guinea pig to come to the front of the class and take an educated guess as to what the item signified. Sometimes he'd want us to try on a piece of clothing and model it. Or, in one of the worst-case scenarios, he'd request that we perform with him in some shame-inducing musical number. Whenever he was in one of his festive, bicultural moods I tended to look down at my feet, hoping he'd resist the temptation to involve me.

Mr. Panna brought in an album from a popular Spanish singer. He took a flouncy red-and-yellow zigzagged shirt from his gym bag and put it on over his already sweaty shirt and then stood in front of the class. "José!" he cried out. *"José! Por favor!* José, don't pretend you don't hear me. Get your fanny up here and take this album from my hand and place it on the record player in the back of the room. *¿Comprende?*"

"*Sí*," said José in a barely audible tone. "José," better known as Joe Eddy, was a tall, well-proportioned sophomore who wore a jean jacket and jeans everyday like a uniform. He rarely looked up from his Converse sneakers. I'd asked Joe to the prom, and he didn't say a word. He was so shy that his sister had to find me and tell me no.

Joe moped to the front of the class, took the album from Mr. Panna, and went to the back of the room to put it on the record player. Mr. Panna put his arm around an invisible waist, took an invisible hand, and started a slow mambo-type step. As if he telepathically read my disgust, he came over to the corner of my desk, still dancing with the invisible someone, and requested, "Laudita, come dance with me."

"No!" I gasped, mortified. "No, thanks. I don't know how to dance."

"Yes, you do, Laudita. *Yo lo vi con mis propios ojos en el teatro.*" He grabbed my fingers and tried to pull me from my seat. I wriggled my hand away.

"Please, get away." I put my hands up as if I could block him out. And then he grabbed both of my forearms and started pulling me up from my seat. I kept myself planted for as long as I could, like a dog using its weight against the tug of a leash.

la ganadora 41

"Lauda, stop it! What's wrong with you. Just have one dance with me."

I gave up and let my body go limp. He was still pulling on me hard, and when I took a step forward, he fell against the chalkboard. The class laughed.

"Are you happy, Lauda?" he asked as if to make me feel guilty. I knew he was about to go into one of his comedy bits. "Are you happy that you threw me against the wall and nearly broke my back?"

Now I started to laugh because of the absurdity of the situation. "Yes, I'm happy. Let's dance and get it over with."

When Mr. Panna put his hand on my waist, a few of the students responded with "oooooohs" as if we were an item.

"Oh, shut up, you animals," Mr. Panna laughed and looked at me. "The lovely Laudita is just demonstrating a dance with me."

I felt myself turning red. He whisked me around in front of the class, and I stepped on his feet a couple of times trying to keep up. When it was over, he twirled me into my seat and bowed, "*Gracias*, Lauda," and waited.

"Well?"

"Oh Christ, *de nada, de nada*," I said with an embarrassed laugh.

Despite the occasional humiliation, Mr. Panna himself, and the peripheral hell all around me, I was starting to learn how to speak Spanish. My bilingual side was just beginning to blossom. One brisk October day, Mr. Panna stood in front of the class looking shockingly professional in a three-piece suit. He took out tiny bifocals, which I'd never seen him use, put them on his face, tallied the attendance and grades for our tenth-grade class with a small calculator, and then snapped his grade book shut.

"I am very proud and honored to announce the winner of the scholarship to Madrid. This person not only had outstanding test scores but in this entire year has only missed my class once—and I'm sure it was for something very, very important."

"Get on with it," Dave Jaffey called out.

"Well, Mr. Jaffey, now that you interrrupted me, I can tell you that you were close, but because you are so rrrrotten"—Mr. Panna's favorite word was "rotten"; he talked to us like we were puppies—"you didn't win. The winner is the sweet Laudita."

Dave Jaffey groaned, and a few of the students next to me patted me on the back and said, "Congratulations."

"What do you think of this, Laudita?"

I was truly thrilled, but I didn't want anyone to think I had tried. I just said, "It's cool."

" 'It's cool' says the humble winner of the scholarship to Spain," Mr. Panna teased me. The scholarship meant the world to Mr. Panna because he put up the money for it him-

 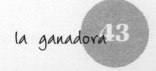

self. It was to encourage students who didn't have the money, even after the assistance of the AFS program, to travel abroad.

"All right, everyone, try and behave. Laudita and I will be right back. We are going to Mr. Vaskey's office to announce la ganadora over the PA system. I guess most of you don't know what I just said, but try and translate it with your pea-sized brains while I escort my one and only outstanding student to the main office." He laughed at the show he was putting on. "Come on, Lauda," he said, grabbing my wrist and facing the door. "Prepare to make your acceptance speech."

"Jeeezus!" Dave Jaffey called out. "It's only three hundred bucks."

"No, it isn't, Mr. Rrrrrotten," Mr. Panna corrected. "It's the flight to Spain and three hundred dollars, making the total scholarship value approximately *un mil quinientos.* You can ask one of your classmates what I just said."

"I know what you said," Dave sulked.

"Well, then, you can win next year if you get your grades up and stop being sooo rrrrrrrotten!" Mr. Panna laughed at himself and dragged me out of the classroom. He led me down the hall and to the stairs, remaining in my ear the entire distance, telling me about the restaurants that I'd love and about the discotheques that I'd never see the insides of because I was too young. And how wonderful it would be for me to reconnect with Christina, my Spanish sister.

All of a sudden I wasn't as thrilled about winning.

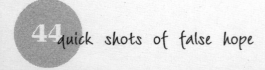

"Wait, I'd have to stay with the same girl who stayed with me?"

"Of course, that's the procedure, *disparatado.* She sees how you live in Los Estados Unidos, and you see *cómo ellos viven en España.*"

"Oh, well, we didn't exactly hit it off."

"*Christina y su familia son muy, muy excitado para verlo.* Don't tell anyone, but I knew that you won yesterday and I contacted the Christina del Marcoses, and they are ecstatic about your visit. *Extático tener a la americana real, la princesa Laudita, en su casa en la playa.*"

"On the beach?" I asked.

"Yes, I'm told *es muy pasmoso.*"

"Oh, they're loaded, huh? No wonder she was so bummed when she stayed with me."

"*¿Lauda, lo que es adentro que es importante, sí?*"

"Um, it's the thought that counts?"

"No. Look it up!"

When we got to the first floor, which was completely empty because we were between classes, we saw someone approaching us. It was my mother—although I didn't recognize her at first. Mr. Panna did, though.

"Mrs. K, this is incredible! You're just in time!" he oozed. He always addressed my mother as "Mrs." even though he knew she wasn't married. When we got closer I could see that my mom had black mascara streaks on her cheeks.

"Mrs. K, are you all right?"

"Yes," my mom squeaked, but she was still half crying, "I have some bad news." I felt sick. I knew what she was going to tell me: Our dog, Chiffon, had died.

"Laura's father has passed away," my mom said as if the news were meant for someone else. It was as if it wasn't my news. Just digesting that very sentence amid the dull hum of the fluorescent lights in the long, white, hospitallike halls of my high school felt like a fake. At that moment I felt a booming nothing and knew I couldn't let it show. I didn't feel sad (even in light of how badly my mom was taking it). I didn't feel happy. I just felt relieved that it wasn't my grandma or Chiffon. Somehow I found the words that I should say. Maybe because I'd heard them on TV since no one in my family or in my circle of friends had ever died.

"Oh, God!" I said. "What happened?"

"He had a heart attack," my mom said.

"Oh," Mr. Panna said. "Oh, well, I'm sorry, Mrs. K." Mr. Panna looked at me. "I'm sorry, Laura." He went on, "I was just going to call you, Mrs. K. I thought maybe you were here because you knew about the scholarship."

"No," my mom said, visibly confused.

"Laura is an outstanding student, and she has won my scholarship fund to go to Spain," Mr. Panna bragged.

"Oh, that's great."

"Well, I should let the two of you go," he said. "Laura,

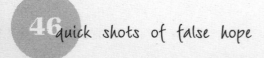

quick shots of false hope

I'll notify the registrar that you won't be attending the rest of your classes." He must have felt like he'd won the gossip jackpot, what with a distraught mistress and a fatherless scholarship winner.

My mom and I drove around the circular high-school driveway. I thought this part of my life would go in slow motion, like I would remember the song on the radio when I got in the car, and I'd remember the first thing my mom said as we drove away from the school. As luck would have it, these would be as forgettable and anticlimactic as the news itself.

"So," I said to my mom, once we were out of the school lot, "a heart attack from what?"

"He was at the YMCA, and he overdid it, I guess."

"Yeah, I guess," I said.

I tried to make myself cry and failed.

Months later, I tried to cry again when I was leaving my Spanish family in Vigo, where I had stayed for three weeks on Mr. Panna's scholarship fund. They were all crying. I guess they'd gotten attached to me. They stuffed me. They showed me off, murmuring, *"muy alta"* (very tall) everywhere we went. As an AFS family, we dined at many an upscale restaurant, where Christina's dad would undoubtedly know somebody— be it the presidente del banco or the sauce steward. I smiled politely when he'd show me off and say, *"Muy alta."* Depending on how much wine he had, a *guapa* (meaning good-looking) was sometimes thrown in. Most everyone smiled or

laughed when my Spanish dad said *muy alta* because I was very tall to almost everyone. In fact, at times I imagined myself as a friendly giant, pounding a hole into the ground with every step, then stopping to watch the little people jump into my footprints.

Other than my Spanish dad's random compliments, I wasn't getting much "play" in Vigo—even though it was a well-known fact that American girls put out. Plus, my Spanish sister, Christina's, friends seemed to be above getting to know an American. I didn't see Christina much, and I didn't like her much. She took me to social get-togethers only because she had to. Which I understood, considering I left her home with my mother while I went to parties, when she stayed with me in Los Estados Unidos.

One week before I was scheduled to go back home, we met four of her friends for lunch at a small café in the center of the city. One of them, a blond Spaniard named Juan-Carlos, was the most affable teen I'd met since I'd been there. He was genuinely interested in me and what upstate Nueva York was like. He understood very, very little English. And my Spanish "sister" was such a little snit that I didn't even want to speak what basic Spanish I knew for fear of sounding like an American idiot and embarrassing her. Juan-Carlos asked me a few questions, and I answered him in fractured Spanish. Still, he was very eager to get to know me, and he made me feel special. He asked me a long question, and I couldn't decipher

quick shots of false hope

any part of it. I turned to Christina, who spoke perfect English. "Christina, what did he ask me?"

Christina gave me a look as if to say, "Shouldn't you try and figure it out? Since you're here to learn Spanish."

I ignored her look and pleaded with her. "C'mon, Christina, I can't understand everything. What did he say?"

She sighed and took a sip of her Coke. In that instant, I thought about choking her in front of her friends. It would be a viable way to get a quick ticket back home and not have to put up with such bullshit. Finally Christina graced me with an answer—but not before she rolled her eyes and giggled with one of her girlfriends.

"Laura," she condescended, "he asked if people can go snow sledding in the streets in the wintertime."

"Well, Jesus, that was a hard one, Christina! How the hell could I ever guess that he was asking me about snow sledding in the streets? And by the way, you can tell your friend, it's just 'sledding'; you don't say 'snow' first. That would be like saying 'water swimming.'"

She smiled and laughed a little bit. There were times when she seemed to get a kick out of me in spite of herself. By the time I was done complaining to Christina, I had forgotten Juan-Carlos's question and felt too put upon and just too fucking brain-dead to keep trying to converse. He was looking at me with a smiling, expectant face. And I left his face sticking out there waiting for a response while I got up to play a selection on the jukebox. I was thinking about how far I'd traveled to be unpopular and how I could have done that just as easily at home. I stood at the jukebox and stared at the selections for as long as I could, dreading the moment when I'd have to go back to our table. I saw the Rolling Stones album, *Tattoo You*, and it looked just like an old friend. I played "Start Me Up," then danced to it by myself, making a conscious decision to get so into my own dance that Christina would cringe. I was boldly taking up most of the café floor, smiling to myself and spinning into *Saturday Night Fever* stances. Christina's friends started laughing and clapping. I danced over to their table and wiggled my ass in their faces. They clapped harder for me. I felt I had won over Christina's snobby friends with my inappropriate behavior, but I still wasn't having a good time.

I didn't have a good time until the night before I left.

Christina and I were going to a party thrown by a friend of hers. She told me that there would be a boy at this party that she would die to go out with, that his name was Enrique, and that she'd had a crush on him for three years. She was the happiest that I'd seen her in the month and a half since we'd met. Before the party we helped each other get dressed in her bedroom and talked about boys. Normally if we were going somewhere together, I'd get dressed in my room and she'd get dressed in hers, and we'd meet in the living room.

When we got to the party, I instantly felt out of place.

quick shots of false hope

Christina told me it was a bit formal. By "formal" I didn't know that she meant like a debutante ball. So I was American and underdressed. What else was new? She didn't seem ashamed of me at this particular party, though. In fact, she was smiling and showing me off to everyone, including the man of her dreams.

Enrique was exactly like she'd described him: medium build, thick black hair, light-brown eyes, and terribly self-assured and sexy for a sixteen-year-old. Enrique brought us beer in plastic cups. This made me so homesick, I thought I might cry. I hadn't seen frothy ale in a plastic cup, or any of life's white-trash pleasures, since I'd left twenty-two days prior. We all clicked our plastic cups, and Enrique and Christina toasted me. I had never seen Christina bring a drop of alcohol to her lips. She drank it fast and hooked her arm around my elbow and started treating me like we were old pals. Enrique kept getting beers. During one of his trips to the kitchen, I told Christina that I would go out and talk to someone on the balcony so that she could be alone to make out with Enrique. She begged me not to. She said she was too afraid to be alone with him.

At some point I realized that I was having trouble with both languages. I was so drunk that I couldn't remember what language I was supposed to be fluent in. I had nearly nodded off on the couch when I saw Christina standing in front of me, leaning on my knees with her hands. She was as drunk

 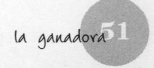

as I was, and she announced: "Come on, the very tall, we've got to go home now."

"Great," I laughed.

Enrique helped us outside to his car and then drove us to Christina's house. I was looking out the window in the back seat and marveling at the majestic hills that seemed to be more blue than green and the purple sky and wondering if I'd remember where we were if I were to ever come back and find this place again. When we got to Christina's home, I got out first and said, *"Gracias, Enrique, de nada."* Or, "Thank you, Henry, you're welcome." I walked away from the car and looked at the stars for a minute, and then Christina came up behind me in a state of elation that I could feel when she put her arm around my waist and we stumbled along the walk together.

"So, you kissed, I hope," I said.

"Yes! Yes!" she said, jumping up and down.

"Great!" I said, tripping and falling to both knees. We both laughed.

Christina helped me up, and then the sheer weight of me on her tiny shoulders knocked her down. We both lay on our backs in the pebbled pathway to her parents' doorstep, weak from laughter and alcohol, and watched the stars.

"I am going to miss you, Laura," Christina said.

"I'll miss you, too," I replied, stunned that we were

quick shots of false hope

actually having this AFS moment that I'd heard so much about.

The next morning Christina and I were completely hung over—and we looked it. At breakfast, Christina's mother asked us how long we stayed at the party. I said, "A few minutes too long" in what I thought was virtually spotless Spanish. They all laughed.

On the drive to the airport I promised Christina and her family that I'd write. I'd grown fond of them, but I was ready to go home. I missed my mom too much to stay any longer.

Vigo was a beautiful place, but with the exception of the last few days there, I hadn't felt very comfortable. I'd spent most of my time at the beach with Christina's nine-year-old sister, Elizabeth, who asked too many questions and took stuff out of her nose and ate it—I'd read *Crime and Punishment* three times that summer just to keep from looking at her. I had really liked Christina's mother. She was one of the kindest people I'd ever met. Every morning at seven A.M. she'd ask, *"Toalla? Toalla, Lauda?"* And every morning I'd say, "Yes, I'd like a towel."

I managed to fake cry at the airport. Then I ran to my seat on the plane.

Good Money

Joelle, a cherubic forty-year-old divorcé with a little-girl voice, would meet my mom for drinks from time to time. They'd go out, looking for fun or companionship or attention or something to soak up the lonely evening hours. I think their nights on the town were a conscious effort to keep their hopes up on the love front; if that wasn't achieved, then at least they had gotten dressed and left the house. That's a tough hurdle to jump, no matter what your mental state.

Joelle was trying to set my mom up on a date with her older brother, Bud. Bud was about forty-three at the time, and my mom was about thirty-two. Bud was quiet. I think the word "sensitive" was thrown around a few thousand times when his name came up.

I remember meeting Bud at Joelle's cousin's house. Joelle's cousin, Viv, was a wealthy real estate agent, thrice divorced and so tan that her epidermis was the color and texture of a gingerbread cookie. Viv was the first woman I'd ever seen with three diamond rings on both ring fingers and several diamond necklaces, all worn at the same time. A walking, yacking gingerbread woman besotted with diamonds and black circles where her eyes were supposed to be. She invited me, my mom, Joelle, and Bud over for leftover cake from her son's birthday party. My mom and I were invited for leftovers so often, it was almost like a side job we held together.

Viv's sons were my age, thirteen or fourteen, and had straight platinum-blond hair and lightly tanned skin. They were friendly and tall and thin and so good-looking that it made me nervous to be around them. My mother told me to play Ping-Pong with Jeff and Daniel, and I did, but my awareness of my plainness was affecting my game. I felt that if they had looked a little more like me or I looked a little more like them, I could have won a few rounds instead of consistently dropping the ball and self-consciously giggling through most of it.

Bud was their uncle. He was on the heavy side, not unattractive but probably not good-looking ever. If, as in a Greek myth, a person could be transformed into the object that they resembled most, Bud would become either a hat rack or a doorstop—useful and unassuming, practical and forgettable. Bud had been born looking like someone's uncle: balding, potbellied, plaid slacked, and sweater vested. Curiously, he had never been married, although he was a nice guy who made "good money." (I thought "Good Money" should have been the name of our town because that's all anyone talked about.) He could've even been considered a catch. The only thing that was really wrong with Bud from the potential-husband standpoint was that he was gay. No one knew that that was an option because in a small town there weren't any gay males, and you didn't even know the word "gay." The word was "bachelor."

Bud was a bachelor. He'd been in a few relationships that didn't work out, and you often heard about his long-term girlfriend, Something Something. When Bud walked out of a room, all of the innumerable, unmemorable excuses for a forty-three-year-old man being unattached were bandied about.

My mother had a few obligatory dates with Bud. I knew nothing was going to happen. Mom's type seemed to be unavailable first and, with the exception of my father, good-looking second. Bud was available and polite. I used to look for Bud's Achilles' heel when he came over to pick my mom up for a date. I asked him questions that would have driven any other man away: Did he ever feel like killing anyone? Did he ever have aspirations to leave town? Did he think my mother was easy? Could men be with men just as easily as they could be with women? I couldn't break Bud. He was hermetically sealed with patience. So I liked him. But everyone, including Bud, knew that he was too boring for my mother.

Eventually my mother told Joelle that she liked Bud a lot but wasn't "sexually attracted" to him, and she didn't think it could ever be more than a friendship. I'm not sure whether it had dawned on my mother that Bud was gay. Come to think of it, it probably hadn't yet dawned on Bud.

After Bud—or maybe overlapping Bud—a courtship commenced with a very wealthy doctor whose name was either Nels or Wells or Miles, a name befitting a person from another town far, far away from ours. The doctor invited my mother and me to his home for Thanksgiving dinner. She accepted without consulting me first. On Thanksgiving afternoon, I was still trying to get out of going with my mother to meet her latest infatuation and his two children.

"So is he divorced or separated?" I asked my mother with the same routine half interest that I gave each of her suitors.

"His wife died," she said while she stepped into her pantyhose.

"Oh, how did she die?"

"She committed suicide."

"Oh, Jesus, *that's* a good sign, Mom."

"No, they said she was a bit depressed when he married her. She'd been in a few mental institutions."

"How did she do it?"

"What?" My mom obviously didn't want to get into it with me.

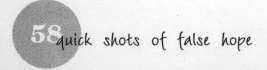

"How did she wait so long to kill herself?" I asked with mock earnest.

"What?"

"For Christ's sake, Mom, how did she kill herself?! Did she do it with sleeping pills?"

"No. Why are you so interested?"

"Death interests me. I want to know what happened, in case, ya know, like, if she poisoned *herself,* maybe you shouldn't drink anything that he makes for you."

"Oh, God, Laura, she was depressed. She asphyxiated herself in the car. She left the gas on," my mom informed me while putting on her mascara with her mouth open.

"I can't believe it doesn't creep you out at all!" I was standing in the bathroom doorway, watching my mother closing her mouth just to dip the applicator back in the mascara goop and then opening it again to do the right eye. "Well, what the hell do you want me to wear to this . . . festive celebration? Ya know, I totally don't want to go. It's sad. Are the kids depressed?"

"No, you'll like his son, Greg. Greg is really cute. He's studying to be a chef."

When we arrived at his house I found that my mom's love interest was a much older, handsome, very Anglo man; in fact, even thinking of him now, all I can see is white. His house was painted white. The walls inside were white, and the furniture was white and tan. I looked around at the framed prints of sailing vessels and thought, "This must be what it's like to be tasteful." It was like swallowing dust. Everything about the place was dry, consistent, well-bred, satisfied; no wonder I felt out of place. I didn't like the doctor's professional demeanor, which he tried to cover with a fake smile, and I couldn't figure out what in hell he was doing with my mother. I guessed he was slumming it, and I didn't want to be there as another representative of that slum. The whole day made me feel like my nails were dirty, like it was a charitable experiment geared toward enhancing the lives of the less fortunate, like taking terminally ill children to Disney World (and letting them wait in lines all day). I wanted to misbehave. I thought it would be funny if I started picking things up and sniffing them. . . .

"What do you call this stuff, Doc? These little fancy leaves? What makes 'em smell so fine? How's that? Po-puree? Mama, ain't the rich funny? They got all these sweet-smellin' leaves in little silver dishes, but they ain't got nothin' to cover up. They ain't got nothin' that stinks like our house." Of course, I didn't do that; but I kept thinking of how to screw things up, either to embarrass my mother or amuse myself or both.

I felt self-conscious for both my mother and myself because my mother wasn't capable of feeling self-conscious on her own. I started hating her and the forced Thanksgiving merriment from the moment the doctor's prissy daughter,

Carolyn, took our coats. Carolyn wore a natural wool dress and pearls. She looked like she had been ordered from a perfect-daughter catalog.

Nels's son, though, didn't seem to belong to him. Greg was my only port in that holiday storm. He was weird and outspoken and determined to have a good time, despite his ice-cold dad and sister. And best of all, he was going to bring me in on it. We were all standing around in the living room, trading awkward glances and getting to know each other on a first-name basis, when Greg rescued me.

"I'd like to show Laura my beer-bottle collection. Is that OK, Dad?"

Nels grimaced at this. His daughter had a similar expression, but hers was more of a sympathetic smile.

My mom laughed. "Oh, sure, go ahead, as long as there isn't any beer left in that collection."

"No," Greg replied, "that's the fun of being a beer-bottle collector. You have to work at it."

My mom and I both laughed at that, and I followed Greg up the stairs. Greg's room didn't look like anything in the rest of the house. There were colors in it. He had an English flag on the wall above his bed, a bong on his desk that was hidden only slightly by a telescope, and something else that I thought was a bicycle pump.

"Your mom seems really cool. What's she doing with an old turd like my father?"

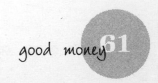

"That's a good question," I responded, and we laughed.

"You're a cute girl, Laura. What do you like to listen to?"

"Led Zeppelin."

"Oh, you're a rock chick, huh?"

"I guess," I said, feeling weird all of a sudden because I was starting to think of Greg in a boyfriend way.

"How old are you?"

"Fifteen. How old are you?" I asked.

"I'm seventeen and about to be stuck in a naval academy or something unless I get accepted into a school for the culinary arts."

"Well, God, I hope you do. I think a naval academy would suck."

"Me, too. Do you cook?"

"No, I don't know how. And neither does my mother. In fact, do you want to hear something sad?"

"Always," Greg said, smiling like he was into me.

"When your dad came over to dinner, my mom asked my aunt to cook something so that my mom could pull it out of the oven as if she'd made it herself."

Greg laughed. "That is so sweet. He doesn't deserve her. I'm always shocked that my dad can even get a date! Can't women tell that he's incapable of love?"

"I guess not. But then again, women are some of the most fucking desperate people I know."

"Yeah," Greg said with a knowing smile, taking a few

extra seconds to look at me like no boy ever had. He leaned forward to gently kiss me. I pulled back—not because I wanted to but because I didn't know what to do next.

"I'm sorry, did I scare you?"

"No, I just didn't expect it."

"Do you like The Who?"

"Yeah."

Greg got up and went over to his stereo and played something from *Quadrophenia*.

"Did you ever see this movie?"

"Yeah, I thought it was great."

"Me, too." Greg put his arm around me and tilted me back against the wall that was flush to his bed, and we kissed again. I was concentrating on the words of the song and trying to relax.

Greg's hands were in my hair and then caressing my back and then his left hand drifted up my side, under my arm and then forward onto my chest, at which point I felt that I had to stop the action.

"Uh, do you think we should see what's going on downstairs?"

"No," he said, still smiling at me and giving me so much attention that I just didn't know what to do with it. "You're really cute, Laura. You've got great eyes."

"Thanks," I said. "I like you, too, but, um, I just feel like this is weird."

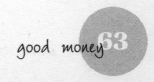

good money 63

"OK, I don't have to touch you. . . . I could just adore you from afar if that's—"

Greg was interrupted by Carolyn's voice. "Greg and Laura, we're about to serve dinner."

"Thanks, slut," Greg said back in a whisper for my amusement. I smiled.

"Greg?" Carolyn called again.

"Be right down!" Then under his breath, "Bitchy-poo." We laughed and Greg kissed me again quickly and kept on with his joke: "On our way witchy-puss. . . . Right there, daddy's girl. . . . Can't wait, crusty-crust."

As we rushed down the stairs, all of this had me laughing like hell. I decided that I liked him a lot. I was even glad I'd shown up.

When we all sat down to dinner, the two women— my mom and Carolyn—served a spicy squash soup that Greg had made.

"Greg," my mom said directly after her first spoonful, "this is fantastic."

"I'm glad you like it. If you finish it, you can have some more."

"Oh, Greg," Nels said, not comprehending the humor. "Mary doesn't have to finish it."

"Oh, I plan on finishing it," my mom laughed. Greg just sipped his wine and smiled, ignoring his father like he had been doing it for years.

quick shots of false hope

"So, Mary," Greg continued, knowing he had found an ally, "Dad said you work at the phone company. Are you the one who gets to disconnect people?"

"Well, no, I'm the one who listens to people beg to stay connected. My assistant is the one who cuts them off." My mom laughed at her own joke.

Greg smiled at me and raised his fist. "Yes! The power to delegate! The smart ones don't get their own hands dirty! Of course, Mary, of course. Your assistant lowers the boom, and you give the sympathetic ear. Do you say, 'Yes, I'll see what I can do'?" He then looked at an imaginary assistant and made the cutting-the-throat gesture with his finger.

My mom and I laughed out loud at Greg's imitation. Greg's sister laughed quietly while she straightened the napkin in her lap. She laughed like it was something she had to do on the sly. We limped along like that despite the fact that the tension in the air between Greg and his dad was a spiderweb that you kept walking into and spent the next few minutes struggling to get out of. Greg was funny—and tragically honest about himself and his relationship with his father. At times I thought Nels was loosening up and ready to cop to being a wet blanket. But he never did. He just laughed in an uptight way. The way people laugh when they want to say, "Shut up."

I think Nels saw my mother one other time after that Thanksgiving Day dinner, then broke it off with her to date an investment banker from another state. Greg called for me once when I wasn't home and talked to my mom for a long time. He told her how lucky she was not to be seeing his father anymore. In September of the following year we found out that Greg had dropped out of the culinary school he was attending in New Orleans and moved back home into his old room, where he hung himself.

quick shots of false hope

Smiles All Around

"So I was wondering if now would be a good time to talk to you about some Ivy League schools," I asked, peeking my head inside the guidance counselor's office. He fell back in his chair laughing, his light-blue fuzzy sweater and yellow checked shirt collar hitting the back of his chair.

"Jesus!" I said. "Watch out. I brought my feelings with me."

He got himself together. "I-I-I'm sorry, Laura," he fumbled. "I thought you were kidding. Ah, you can't get into an Ivy League school. They look at cumulative grade-point average, and they want strong SAT scores."

"Well, doesn't it matter that I was the editor of the newspaper and the president of Drama Club?" I asked, suspecting that it didn't matter.

"Well, extracurricular is important, but you have to have the grades to back it up," he said in a guidance counselory way.

"Oh,"—long pause of thinking about who I could blame for my grades—"well, do you think I could get into Syracuse?"

"Yes, I think you could."

I did get into Syracuse, but when I looked at the campus, I thought I'd get lost there, and anyway it was too expensive, so I went to Fredonia State College instead. My hometown was only about an hour away, and I drove home just about every weekend to see my mom and our dog, Chiffon. I liked Fredonia; it wasn't much of an adjustment from high school. There were girls there who looked like my high-school friends and boys who looked uninterested in me. I signed up for a few different groups like the newspaper and—Actually, I may have just signed up for the newspaper. I was much more interested in social drinking.

At the college newspaper meeting I was assigned the job of "activities" co-editor. A very low-pressure position. Beth, the woman with whom I shared my spunky title, thought it would be fun if students sent in their baby pictures, and we made a contest out of guessing which adorable baby had become which not-so-adorable college student.

I went home the following weekend to get my baby picture for our column. There was a bureau in the dining room where all the photos were kept, and in the bottom drawer—under my high-school graduation photo and my

quick shots of false hope

mother's flight-school photo—I found something that intrigued me.

At first I thought it was one of those tourist photographs taken at Niagara Falls, where you put your face on top of a life-sized cardboard cut out of Richard Nixon's or Marilyn Monroe's body. Yet if it had been one of those photo souvenirs, it was by far the least kitschy and most disturbing one I'd ever seen: the actual naked body of a lady in a yellow vinyl dentist's chair, with my mother's face peering out over the neck. Now, what the hell kind of a tourist attraction was *that?* "You'd have to be hard pressed for fun to get your picture taken in one of those things," I thought. And where had she gone to get it? It could have been taken at one of those little photo stands at the fair where people get their pictures snapped while waiting for ferris wheel tickets. The ones that only offer one male choice and one female choice for a funny photo keepsake like: "Naked Woman in a Dentist's Chair" or "Naked Man in a Sling."

I instinctively looked at the back of the photo as if I'd find scribbled in my mother's familiar block letters: MARY. CHUCK'S OFFICE. 1984. But, of course, there was nothing there. I wasn't supposed to be seeing this, I knew, but I couldn't stop staring at it—it just got better and better. On the wall, in the corner of the dentist's office, above my mom's naked shoulder, was a poster with a rainbow over a field full of butterflies.

Inside the stripes of the rainbow were the words: BELIEVE IN MIRACLES.

I took this as a message that probably wasn't from God. A message to cherish life's outrageously ironic moments—because they were what I could count on. Like, maybe I'd never live comfortably or be considered successful, but in its stead I'd be the one person lucky enough to bear witness to the kind of foibles that aren't the stuff set up on TV shows, that are barely the stuff of normal people's lives. Like the time I opened the door to a friend's apartment building just as an old man tripped down a short flight of stairs and landed on another old man who was sleeping one off in the foyer. What's that worth? Can the experience of walking into that moment be bought?

Although we were close, the "lost nude" made me feel like I didn't really know my mother. I felt I didn't know *anybody.* It was as if I were just stopping by this person's home, observing. My mother wasn't just my mom, she was a woman, an uninhibited nude woman, who had hung out with a really invasive dentist.

"Woo-hoo!" I cried, holding the picture by the corner and waving it like a lottery ticket. I couldn't keep a discovery like this to myself, and since I didn't have any brothers or sisters to share it with, I decided to stand there in the dining room until my mom appeared. I looked away from the photo down at our dog, who was looking at me, and then I looked

quick shots of false hope

up at the plastic chandelier on the ceiling and then back at our dog, showing her the photo. "Look at Mommy, Chiffon." She looked blankly at me. And then I could have sworn she said, "Put it away"—or if not "Put it away," then, "Kill yourself." Finally, Mommy came home and saw me holding the photo.

"What are you doing?" she snapped.

"Well, I was looking for my copy of *National Geographic* and—"

"Where did you get that?"

"In the drawer," I replied matter-of-factly.

She took it from me and threw it into a different drawer.

"Well, that will never bother us again," I said sarcastically. I followed her into the kitchen.

She was trying to be mad at me. "God, Laura, do you always have to have your nose lookin' in everything?"

"Oh, yeah," I drawled. "Like I wanted to find that. Like I came home to do research and wondered, 'Hmmm, where did I come from, *exactly?*'"

And eventually we laughed it off. But I still thought about it. I wondered if Dr. Wisell had given my mother the only souvenir from the You Only Go 'Round Once Phantasmagoria or if he had kept one, too. Maybe he collected nude Polaroids of all of his patients like the sick thrill addicts who collect salt-and-pepper shakers or knick-knack skunks.

This Is Pathetic

I was finding it too easy to go home every weekend, so I transferred from Fredonia to Emerson College in Boston. Plus, I don't think Fredonia was good for me. I'd become too comfortable walking to a college bar and literally crawling on all fours back to my dorm where I'd spend the night passed out in the hall in a fetal position hugging my combat boots.

The cover of the Emerson College brochure featured a cute boy reading under a tree next to a pond with a swan paddle boat on it. I liked that. I pictured myself with that boy countless times and in countless ways. In my thoughts I'd approach him, and he'd throw down his book and run toward me. Within moments we'd be all over that riverbank in all manner of dress and undress, swimming in the water, drinking in the swan boat. I knew I'd exhausted every imaginable position with this unknown student when I imagined him peering up from his book to watch me lying nude with an actual swan. It was for this beautiful stranger that I transferred to Emerson. That and it was the only institution that accepted my transfer application.

My entrée into Emerson was not without its pitfalls. First there was my roommate. She was clean scrubbed, puritanical, and paranoid. She had one friend Shelia, who, like Lacey, hated me instantly. I started referring to them as the Mouse Frumpies—I guess because they were mousy and frumpy and I was a g.d. genius! They were always sewing something. In fact, whenever I entered the room I felt like a robot destroying a Quaker village. This was Lacey's sole companion until she met a boy.

His name was Spencer, and he was a tall glass of acne. He wore khakis and a pink Izod shirt with a yellow sweater tied around his shoulders. Of course, a persnickety flower like Lacey would bring home a gay boyfriend. Not just bring home, but import—from Tarrytown, New York. One night, when I was informed that Spencer might sleep over, I tried to stay out late. But, regrettably, not late enough.

I snuck into my bunk bed and as I was about to doze off, I heard muffled protests from Lacey's partitioned alcove. "Ow, ow, wait, ow, oooh, Spencer, you're going too fast." Then I heard Spencer: "Yeess, innndeeeedy!"

The next morning I woke up cringing. I pretended to be asleep to avoid their goofy postcoital-bliss mugs. When they left the room, I got up and walked into Lacey's sexed-in single. The bed was neatly made with pillows and teddy bears and

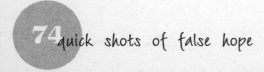

quick shots of false hope

Lacey's lace. I looked up at the Shaun Cassidy poster. Oh, to be a smiling pop flop on the wall when that heinous act went down. Yeess, innndeeedy.

As the weeks passed, our living situation became more and more uncomfortable, what with the tense silence between us and Shaun Cassidy's unyielding senseless grin; my eyes seemed to fall upon that grin at the most inopportune moments, like when I was on the hall phone looking into our room to see if she was there to hear me talking about her, or sniffing an article of clothing to make sure it stunk, or surveying my behind in Lacey's full-length mirror. At some point I'd catch that breezy smile and think, "Stop smiling at me, you fuckin' jackass!"

In short, Lacey and I were not meant to cohabitate, but neither of us wanted to leave. We were in a plum spot in the center of college life on Beacon Street with a second floor walk-up that freed us from ever using the old service elevator; and we could sit on our fire escape and watch everyone walk to class—although you wouldn't want to sit out there unless you were wearing something black or ripped.

I met my new friend Dana in a creative-writing class. Dana and I were inseparable. We ate together, shopped in Kenmore Square together, hustled tricks together. We actually didn't hustle tricks but I would have if she wanted to. As it happened, Dana hated her roommate, too, so we started plotting a way to share a room.

In a rare moment of lucidity, I took action. While Lacey was spending the weekend in Tarrytown, I put a noose around the neck of one of her teddy bears and hung it from the ceiling over her bed. When she came home and found it, she requested a transfer out of our room and eventually went to a different school.

Dana was an actress. At Emerson, there were a lot of people who took acting classes and "movement" classes and musical theater classes and just assumed they'd float into an acting-movement job when they graduated. I don't think anyone there was ever dogged by the thought of having to get a real job after college. They were counting on the college production of *Candide* to open doors for them. I, on the other hand, was taking a more practical route. I took courses in writing, film, and television production. Dana was the first person to dash my hopes of a steady nine to five existence. She told me about "This Is Pathetic," a comedy troupe that she was auditioning for, and asked me if I wanted to try out, too. I wrote something to audition with and took some broad, conventional stabs at character impressions like: a zealous cheerleader and a horny nun. I didn't get in the troupe. Dana also got nixed.

But when we auditioned again the following year, I got a bit more imaginative with my characters and felt a communal wave of approval from the members. One of the characters, a neighbor with ultra-sensitive hearing who tortured

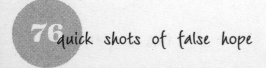

quick shots of false hope

people with her demands, brought applause from the troupe. The audition left me feeling giddy, but I decided to keep my hopes down anyway, so I wouldn't have as far to fall when I wasn't asked to join.

I remember staring at the list that the comedy-troupe members had pinned to the bulletin board in the Student Union. I couldn't stop staring at my own name. Again and again I read the list as if each time was the first time—like I just happened to see it while I was looking for voice lessons or an ad to buy a used amp. I approached the list from different angles in the Student Union, like ambling down the stairs and pretending to find it and running past it and backing up to read it, putting my finger under my own name as if there could be another person with a name nearly identical to mine that I was confusing myself with. The list seemed short to me. I was trying to remember the people that I signed up to audition with, and then I realized I hadn't scanned the list for Dana's name. Alphabetically, her name should have been directly after mine—and it wasn't. After me it went straight to Plummer. "Oh, shit," I thought. And just as I was turning to leave, I caught Dana bounding up the Student Union steps.

"Is it up?" she asked.

"Uh, yeah," I said as if I'd been caught with something.

"Well, I obviously didn't get it or you'd be congratulating me."

I stood there trying to think of a witty reply as she stepped in front of me to read the list.

She ran her finger down the list, then turned to me and gave me a hug. "Whoa! Congratulations, roomie!" I thought she held on to me for a minute too long to brace herself. When she pulled away, I could see that her eyes were watery.

"Well, I guess I'll have to try again next year," she muttered. "You think you can get me in?"

"It's done," I said, attempting to erase the look of sympathy that I knew was on my face.

"Well, I should go. I'm going to be late for my next class, losers one-o-one."

"Oh, c'mon, Dana, it's a stupid comedy troupe. . . ." I stopped myself before I said something else that sounded like a false blanket consolation.

She backed off the Student Union steps and pointed at me. "No, it isn't a stupid comedy troupe, and congratulations—you funny bitch!"

"You wanna go to dinner?" I asked.

"Can't. I'm going out with Doug."

"OK, I'll see you later."

She waved good-bye and walked briskly across the intersection to Commonwealth Ave. I knew exactly how she felt. Walking away with all the hurt lodged in her throat, then running until she found the right place to cry her head off.

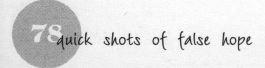
quick shots of false hope

And I couldn't believe that it wasn't me who was walking away crestfallen. I'd been asked to partake in this exclusive comedy circle that would ensure my happiness from this day forward. How was it possible? I didn't care—I felt pretty.

A month into joining the troupe, as if on cue, I was getting noticed. Some of my classmates would come up to me and tell me how funny they thought I was in the show. Once I knew popularity with all the trimmings I didn't know how I'd gone for so many years without it.

I started losing weight and wearing pajama bottoms and T-shirts to class, in effect telling the world, "I'm ready for love and guess what, I'm already half-dressed for it." In fact, there wouldn't be a style I hadn't tried by the time I entered my junior year. I dyed my hair orange, pink, red, black, teasing it at the roots so it came straight out of the crown of my skull and splayed down over my face like a fountain. I was doing The Cure look with as much if not more conviction than they were. Not to mention, everyone at Emerson was plunging into new looks. It was as if we'd been given ten minutes to come up with a new identity and we all scrambled to the same box of black eyeliner and hairspray.

It was a sophomore named Joe who had started the troupe that was fast becoming my ticket to acceptance.

He was a tall, thoughtful Irishman who at times was so in his head about sketch and film ideas that he'd accidentally clunk into people on the street and then take his hat off and bow an apology. I had heard about Joe even before the Pathetic auditions and when he returned, there was a buzz around campus. (It was the actual sound of buzzing, but only I could hear it.) Everyone knew who Joe was. I'm not saying that one twenty-year-old could make the campus unified, but sometimes it felt that way.

The first time I saw him was in the elevator. He was wearing a tweed blazer, sweatpants and an Irish fisherman's cap. He had shoulder-length light-brown hair and orblike clear blue eyes. He didn't notice me. I thought about introducing myself, so he would know that I was a member of the group he started, but I decided to wait until the next meeting, which would be his first upon returning from his semester in L.A. Watching him fidget with his blazer and tap a tune out to himself on his leg was the sort of elevator behavior of a hard doer, I thought. Most people just look up.

When Joe and I were introduced at the *This Is Pathetic* meeting, he hugged me and said "Welcome." That was all I needed. That friendly embrace kick-started the crush. At the subsequent rehearsals together, I was blown away by how easy it was for Joe to embody a character, be it a mentally retarded child, a French maid, or an old, deaf sea captain— whatever it was, he made it seem as fun and easy as a game of hopscotch.

Joe eventually became aware of my interest in him and started to reciprocate: we found ourselves making excuses to

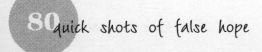

see each other in the guise of working out sketches for the troupe. On one of our "writing dates," he told me that he'd had his heart broken by his first love, Jennifer, and that I was the first person he'd liked in a while.

Pretending to be in the area, I stopped by his apartment one night. We drank tea and watched the end of a movie together. I was in his bathroom with the door open, arranging my stiff locks like a florist filling out a bouquet, when he walked in behind me and put his arms around my waist. "Wow," I thought as I looked at both of our faces in the mirror, "I am truly in love." We had sex soon after, and when I got up in the morning, I tripped on the phone cord which brought the phone and the lamp on his nightstand crashing to the floor. He laughed and came up with a pet name for me: the swan.

When Joe graduated, we were still dating and in love. The troupe wasn't as much fun without him in it and my thoughts gravitated to stand-up. Joe came to the clubs a few times to see me, but it made him so nervous that I told him he didn't have to come. He wasn't a fan of "standing still and telling jokes," but he really admired me for doing it. He started working full-time in a mailroom at a law firm to pay off his college loans and was getting tired of working late and not having enough time to write. Our near-perfect romance was beginning to feel the strain of the outside world. And the more Joe recoiled, the more I glommed on.

For my graduation, the following year, Joe surprised me with a stunning garnet ring shaped like a flower with tiny pearls outlining the petals. Since we were fighting on a semi-regular basis, the present really floored me.

In July a fellow comic told me about a psychic he knew. I thought she might provide some insight as to what would become of my B.S. degree. Actually, I was feeling encouraged because of how well my stand-up sets were going and I thought I'd ask her when I'd "make it."

When I called her the first thing she said was, "Every time I see you, your hair is a different color." I thought that was unbelievable because I had changed my hair color so often I'd been asked by my hairstylist to stop. Not to mention this seer had never met me. I was deeply impressed.

She told me a few other things I can't remember and asked me if I had any questions. I asked her if Joe and I would move in together. There was an unbearably long pause, and then she said, "I don't think you'll be seeing the young man that you are currently seeing for much longer."

I gasped, "Oh, no, that can't be true! We're probably going to get married. We're soul mates." But she was right.

A few weeks after the call, Joe went to New York to attend a science-fiction film marathon. He and his friend Jim made this trip annually, and to me it sounded like torture. Endless screenings of sci-fi hits and misses, from *Plan 9 From Outer Space* to *Escape From the Planet of the Apes* and the point of this survival game was not to leave. Joe would come home from these marathons bragging about how he didn't get up to pee for a certain number of hours. And that his butt was sore.

On this particular trip, I had a hunch that he was doing more than sitting for hours on end. The day that Joe was to return from New York, I went to his apartment to put flowers on the table and clean the place up before he got there. I really hadn't planned to clean his journal, but it was in his closet, and I saw it when I was putting his clothes away. Because of our steady bickering of late and because of the psychic reading, I couldn't resist. I had to take a glance.

"I fell on my knees when I had to leave her"—I read, touched that he felt such anguish over leaving me; I turned the page—"and go back to *L*." For a long moment that didn't register. "Who or what was the 'L' that he dreaded coming back to? Was it 'law firm'?" I wondered, knowing how much he hated his job; then both palms flew to my chest as if I were pressing an emergency button, and I gasped for air as I fell back into his closet, knocking down his shirts and landing hard on his sneakers; I realized that "leave her" was leaving his first love, Jennifer, who he must've been seeing on his visits to New York! And coming back to "L" meant returning to the dungeon keeper—me. I sat on his shoes and cried. When the physical discomfort was too great, I got up and cried on his bed. "I deserve this for invading his privacy," I

thought. I spent the next few hours waiting for him, trying to decide if I should broach the topic of Jennifer.

When he walked in the door, I was really glad to see him. We kissed, and I imagined that there was something different, something obligatory, about the kiss. I really needed to heighten the drama for myself. Without even letting him unpack, I jumped in with both feet to ruin it. "So, how was New York? Did you see Jennifer?"

"What? Why would you ask me that?" he barked, racking his brain for an excuse, while trying to deflect me. "Did someone mention to you that I might have?"

I uncoyly said that one of our mutual friends had hinted around about it. But rather than have him torture all of his friends like he said he would to get an answer, I admitted to reading part of his journal. He was furious. He told me he did still have feelings for her, and maybe we shouldn't see each other. A few calls from me crying and screaming with things like "Well, you won, Joe" and "I'm going to hang myself" followed.

I could lie on my bed and cry for hours back then. Just wail, stop, and then start myself back up again with the surging twenty-four-hour remorse that accompanies first-love heartache.

Big

I was doing stand-up at Stitches in Boston, performing at other clubs on open-mike nights. Amateur night was a chance for new comics to feel their balls freeze up inside their stomachs. For the open-mike audience, it meant laughing hard for a friend or pity laughing for someone when it became uncomfortable not to laugh. In any event, it was handled in a completely humane way, with a seasoned comic emcee asking the audience to be kind and supportive to these people who were backstage freaking out.

After watching beginners, headliners, and old relics I became aware of a huge dividing line. There were the good comics who walked on stage with original, thought-provoking material that they'd written themselves, and there were the hacks. The hacks never joked outside of their typical-premise milk-fed-veal pen. If their jokes weren't blatantly lifted from Richard Pryor or George Carlin, there'd be an aftertaste of someone else's persona when they left the stage. Most audiences will laugh at derivative comedy because, like an old song on a soft-rock station, unoriginality will prevail at timed intervals on an endless loop.

My social life existed almost entirely inside the beer-soaked perimeters of the Stitches comedy club. I got to know everyone. It was like a small town full of alcoholics trying to be funny. Whenever I heard a comic launch into an observational tidbit about how "there's always that one sock that gets lost in the dryer"—and the subsequent huge "recognition" laugh from the audience—I'd shake my head. After two whole years in the business, I was already above that sort of empty drivel. I knew that kind of idiot would always make more money and get banged by more drunken chicks on the road but I knew I never wanted to be him.

My sounding board on whether I was steering clear of hack territory was two Massachusetts natives, Brian and Bill, two highly regarded stand-ups who raised the expectations of audiences by consistently putting on a smart show. I met them on an open-mike night that Brian was hosting at Catch A Rising Star in Cambridge. They were old friends who started around the same time in the early eighties. It wasn't long before Bill and Brian accepted me into their world—the blessed bitching sessions—the taking up of the bottled beer and the settling down to the business of who sucked and why. This was an important time for me: It nourished the seedling of bitterness that would soon grow into the old rotting tree

quick shots of false hope

of bitterness I knew I could become. Drinking Rolling Rocks with Bill and Brian at Catch A Rising Star in Harvard Square offered some of the longest soul-bearing laughs I've had in my life.

I was discovering that no matter how badly you bombed or how thoroughly you were stripped clean of your self-respect, there was always a comic with a story to out-horror yours. I found a world of comfort in that phenomenon. I was at a bar with a few other comics, telling a story involving my performing for a bachelorette party that would not let me finish a joke, when lo and behold, one of the comics I was drinking with, Mark, told me that I didn't know the meaning of humiliation. He had just performed at a benefit held by the Giant's football team to raise money for terminally ill children. All around the table we were holding our mouths, cradling our stomachs, preparing ourselves for the worst, then someone asked,

"Wait, why would you even take a gig like that?"

"You mean, for dumb old sick kids?" Mark glibly countered.

"Oh, God, yeah. Go on."

"Well, it was transcendent. The truth is, I don't know if I can go back to the old way of bombing. . . ." He paused and took a long sip of his draft beer.

"C'mon you bastard. What happened?" one of the other

comics prodded. We were salivating like a pack of squirrels over the promise of an acorn.

"Well," Mark started gingerly, "after about two minutes into my act, I was getting a couple of boos. I thought, 'This shouldn't be happening at a benefit.' Then it gets louder, so I step out of the spotlight and squint into the audience to see a full row of kids in wheelchairs. I'm being booed off stage by kids with cancer."

Hearing this kind of bad news was like receiving a medal from a war hero. It was something you'd want to keep taking out of your breast pocket and rubbing, when you needed to derive strength to contend with your own miserable shows.

"God bless you," I said, and we lifted our glasses to toast Mark's extraordinary bad luck.

At Stitches, there was a small back room that led to the stage, where a lot of the comics did coke. I did it, too, when invited, though never before a show. I remember one night sitting in the back room with four male comics who were about ten to fifteen years older than I was—some absolute Boston legends, some I idolized. I watched these comics go through two coolers of beer and a couple of grams of coke and a few joints within the course of an evening of comedy. And every one of those fuckers killed on stage. Some even got standing ovations, so maybe I, too, should have been partaking in preshow recreational drugs, but I didn't have the confi-

quick shots of false hope

dence. I was so nervous, anyway, I thought that nervous energy and cocaine energy would be a fatal mix. Or if not fatal, at least terminally unfunny. I remember living with a guy in a band, and when his bandmates came by and did coke, a verbal circle jerk commenced that sometimes lasted up to nine hours. I'd fall asleep overhearing bits of inanity like: "That's what I mean, man; we've got to invest in ourselves!"

One night when they had just brought the cooler of beer into the back room, and Lenny and Mike and Don were passing around their blow mirror, Lenny asked me if I wanted any coke. Since I was about to perform, I told him no thanks. Then as if this was typical small talk, he asked, "So, Laurie, you a rug muncher?"

I didn't even know what it meant. One of the guys laughed.

"Ah, what?" I asked.

"Ya know, a carpet cleaner, a muff diver, a lesbo?"

"Oh." "Lesbo" is a term I had heard. "No, no, I'm not."

"Oh, good. Well, then, good. It's OK if you are. I just wondered 'cuz, you know, there aren't a lot of women doing this, and I didn't see you with a guy or nothin'. I mean, if you are, it doesn't matter. I was just askin', ya know."

"Yeah. Um, I'm not."

In '87 there weren't many female stand-up comics in Boston. It was a Thursday night, and I had been much appreciated by the audience—at least that's what it felt like. I wasn't embraced but I was given the equivalent of a warm handshake, and to me, that was plenty. In the audience was Barry, a comic and combative liberal. Barry knew so much about history and foreign policy and human rights issues that you'd often see audience members watching his performance with their yaps stuck open wondering what the hell they were missing. He was so well-informed on world events, I lived in fear he'd ask me what I thought about anything. So I didn't say much when he was around.

He approached me after my set and shocked me by requesting that I perform at his "year-in-review" show the following week. To which I slobbered out, "Wow! Yeah, I'd love to! Thanks, Barry!"

On the night of Barry's show, my insides, specifically stomach and bladder, were making me pay for this stand-up upgrade. (A debt I'd never settle, as it turns out.) So much so, that I thought I'd be listening to my intro from a bathroom stall.

Barry brought me up on stage with such heartfelt praise, I perceived my act to be better than it was.

I had one of the strongest sets I had ever had in that club—perhaps because the room was full of Barry followers who could not let him down by dismissing me.

After the show, a petite, attractive blond woman came over to me. Barry was right behind her and he introduced us. Her name was Cynthia. She shook my hand heartily and

quick shots of false hope

said, "Laura, you were great! Your material is very provocative and dark. I really liked your style up there." And the next compliment she gave in the way of a nod of approval to Barry, "And she's very pretty, too."

I felt like I was wagging my tail next to my owner, having just won Best Bitch at the dog show. She asked if she could contact me for club dates in New York. I gladly gave her my number, not knowing exactly what she meant. I didn't know you could just be given work at a club; I thought there must be some kind of punishment involved—a long sign-up line, a few auditions, a brisk crack with a pair of nunchucks. Well, nunchucks would have been the sweet alternative to what was coming.

I arrived in Manhattan on a Saturday afternoon and planned on staying with Linda, one of my college buddies. When I took the subway to Catch A Rising Star that night, I had a feeling I'd probably slay 'em. I got to the club, and the door guy gave me a bit of grief before letting me in. "Shit," I thought, "that asshole is going to be sorry." Looking at all of the photographs of stand-ups that lined the walls just added to my bogus bout of confidence. Staring at Freddie Prinze's photo on the wall—and probably being the same age as he had been when the photo was taken—I felt it was an omen. "I'll ask Cynthia to put my photo next to his when I get one," I thought. I was there on a Friday night. The fact that I had never done well on a weekend night didn't faze me. This was

New York City. This audience would be looking for the next big thing; they were waiting for me to rock their world.

The place was packed, stuffy from the smoke and filled from wall-to-wall with partygoers. I looked at the crowd from offstage, and they seemed to be a mix of tourists—not nearly as stylish as I wanted them to be; in fact, they looked like people from my hometown. Still, I went on stage feeling immeasurably talented and after two minutes I was dying the slowest death imaginable. As the silences between jokes got longer, I started saying my material faster and faster as if the words themselves could camouflage the audience's despondence. I barely stopped to breathe. I felt like a magician at a child's birthday party who was running out of tricks to keep their attention. There wasn't a thing up my sleeve that these people wanted. Then a drunk goaded on by his friends at a table far away from the stage began heckling, "Who are you? Are you Gilda Radner?" It was the late eighties, and this was an assinine dig because she hadn't been in the public eye for almost ten years, but the audience laughed like mad.

My funny comeback? "No."

"I didn't think so!" he bellowed back. Making the score: heckler, two; sad clown, zero.

I tried to do another joke.

"Hey, are you David Letterman's wife?" the guy taunted. The crowd laughed at him again; some people clapped.

I stumbled through my last joke and muttered, "Good

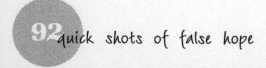

night" to all the high-school bullies who'd grown up to be comedy connoisseurs.

On the train back to Boston, I decided New York audiences were vile and resigned myself to the fact that I would never work at the New York City Catch A Rising Star again. As I was basking in a mild depression back in my apartment, I got a call from Cynthia. "I guess you heard," I told her.

"Yeah," she consoled. "I think weekends can be really rough. I shouldn't have put you on one so soon." I thought that that was the end of our conversation and perhaps our relationship, but she surprised me. "Laura," she said, "there was a person there who liked you very much and would like you to audition for a movie."

"Really?" I asked.

"Do you know who Juliet is?"

"No."

"She casts Woody Allen movies."

"No!" I gulped, instantly picturing myself on a set with Woody Allen.

"Yep. Can you come in this Friday?"

So, I was back on the Metroliner to New York, on my way to audition for the part of the female lead in the upcoming movie, *Big*. (It wasn't a Woody Allen movie, after all.) I remember looking out the window thinking, "Well, this is it.

I had a rough start in New York last week, but this is going to make it all seem worthwhile." Again, I gladly fell into the misleadingly cozy hammock of hope.

When I got off the train, I went with the first cabby to ask me if I needed a ride. I must've looked as from-out-of-town as a jackass possibly could. Eight blocks and twenty bucks later, it was as if I was in a Buster Keaton parody of a bumpkin coming to New York for the first time (although it was my second), as the hordes of people speedwalking to their lunch-hour destinations nearly knocked me over. How the hell can anyone live in a place with so many people? It over whelmed me. Ten minutes before I was due to arrive in Juliet's office, I entered the gold-plated skyscraper lobby and walked around until I found the correct elevator bank.

I was nervous to the point of being struck dumb waiting in the small reception area opposite one white desk with the New York City skyline booming in the window behind it. "I will never forget this view," I thought. I did forget it, though. I can't even remember the address—and this was my very first audition.

Ellen, Juliet's assistant, met me at the door. She showed me to my seat, told me how funny I'd been the other night, and asked if I wanted something to drink. I was taking everything to heart. Every common courtesy had me thinking, "She's kissing my ass; I've got what it takes and they know it."

After about ten minutes alone in the waiting room, I

was introduced to a woman who reminded me of an older Esteé Lauder model with white-blond hair, an unthreatening demeanor, and Nordic features—a Swiss Mrs., if you will.

"Hi, Laura, it's a pleasure to meet you. Ellen was telling me how funny you were the other night at Catch A Rising Star."

"Really? Thanks," I gushed.

"So, Laura, have you had any training?"

I think it must've been obvious that I hadn't because for a minute I didn't know what she meant. I nearly asked, "Training for what?" before I caught myself. "Well, I've had a few, um, theater classes . . . and I'd like to eventually get some film parts. . . ." I covered.

"Well, great. I'd like to have you read something for me today. Now, Laura, let me explain this part. We're casting for a movie called *Big*. It's with Tom Hanks." Since it was still the eighties, I only had a vague idea who Tom Hanks was, so I pretended to be impressed.

"Oh, great!" I replied enthusiastically.

"We're looking for a lead. Someone to play his girl-friend. She has to be—understanding but at the same time frustrated with the fact that the man she loves has turned into a ten-year-old boy. . . ."

I nodded. I was thinking: "I could do this. Every guy I *know* acts like a ten-year-old!"

Juliet told me to go back into the waiting room and

look over the script. I scanned the stage directions and made a mental note that "Beth" was carrying a briefcase that she throws down in a fit of anger. I'd learned in a theater handbook somewhere that paying attention to detail can make or break the scene. After about five minutes, I told Ellen I was ready. She knocked on Juliet's door. "Laura's ready." We walked back in, and Ellen sat in a chair across from me.

"Ellen's going to read with you," Juliet prompted.

I looked around the room for something that looked like a briefcase. I asked Juliet if I could use her date book for the scene.

"Ah, sure," she offered, probably supressing a laugh.

I put the book on the floor next to my chair so that I'd have easy access when the time came. I stared at Ellen for a few seconds, "taking her in," as the professionals would say. We began the scene, which started out low-key. By the second page of dialogue, my character's anger toward the man-child was mounting. I tried to impart the frustration that I'd felt when Joe dropped me.

When I felt my hurt was ready to go, I stood up, hurled the substitute briefcase and screeched, "I can't tell you *anything!*" The book hit the corner of her desk, releasing all of its contents on impact. Naturally, I started retrieving her addresses while still looking at my script and reading my lines. I don't know why I did any of this; I thought I was going to

quick shots of false hope

come off as spontaneous and intense as opposed to clumsy and mentally unfit.

She said, "Well, thank you, Laura, that was very good." I thought she meant it.

I left there feeling pretty goddamned pleased with myself. I thought that by throwing her addresses all over the floor, she'd remember me as the actress who "takes chances."

When I got back to Boston, I called Cynthia. She didn't return my call. So I assumed my audition didn't go as well as I thought. I tried a few times over the following weeks; finally I got her in person, and she told me I might want to consider acting lessons.

Jimmy Archer

I had been living in Manhattan for about a year and was performing in a few clubs in the city when I was asked to do stand-up at an upstate New York college specializing in equestrian studies. The college was near my hometown, so I called my mom and asked her if she wanted to come and visit me there.

When we arrived, a round woman with round glasses and wavy gray hair greeted us in front of the house where we'd be staying. She asked if we performed together. "All of our lives," my mother said. The woman laughed way too hard. She showed us around the mammoth old Victorian mansion and said everything had been preserved to look like it did in 1850 "except for the bean-bag chairs in the living area"— which made her laugh way too hard again. In fact, she laughed so hard that I laughed too hard right back just to see if we both sounded nuts. I was smiling to myself about the fact that she said "living area." I wanted to put my arm around her shoulder and say, "Come on, aren't we all white-trash low-test scorers at a third-rate private school for dykes who want to be vets or vets who want to be dykes?"

She told us that they were having a salute to Margaret Mead and a follow-up "Women in Literature" seminar. There would also be sign-up booths throughout the campus because it was Great Women Writers week.

At this point I was getting sick of the word "women," but then again this just stank of the kind of gig I was used to getting. I usually did shows for almost no money in college cafeterias for freshmen couples who watched me with their heads tilted to one side like bored six-year-olds trying to stare me off stage. Or I'd get the all-female-campus females who listened to me like they were hearing the oracle and laughed at just about everything I said. This was one of those nights.

I embellished without conscience. I felt like Columbus bragging about the New World and leaving out the part about screwing the Indians. When I said the word "fuck," they squealed as if I were handing out bags of heroin in a methadone clinic. After my set, the shy red-headed teenager who had introduced me invited me to share in chips and nonalcoholic beverages. The other young women smiled at me for a second until one extended her hand. "I thought you were really funny. I've seen you on MTV."

quick shots of false hope

"Oh, thank you," I said. Then I felt like an ass for acting so smug on their "stage," which was more like a low buffet table painted black. It was right next to a Ping-Pong table, and I kept referring to it in my act with: "Who says St. Vincent girls don't know how to party!"

My mom joined me and said, "Well they seemed to like you. I don't know why you had to say the F word so much."

"Mom, are you complimenting me in a way?" I asked, not really wanting to get into it with her.

"Yeah, you were good. I'm just sayin' I don't think you needed to say the F word with the teachers there." My mom always stopped a compliment dead in its tracks for me by beginning it with, "I'm just sayin'" . . . Like the time I won the high-school poetry contest and had my poem read on the air by the local morning DJ. When the DJ finished reading my "work," I looked at my mom.

"Well, Mom . . ." I'd said.

"I'm very proud of you," she'd responded. "It sounded really good. I'm just sayin' you should do a couple of them that rhyme. People like hearing things rhyme."

After my highly successful F-word-studded perfor-mance, my mom and I went back to our room. I took a hot bath and got into the king-sized four-poster bed with my mother, who was lying on top of the covers in her nightgown, reading a visitor's brochure.

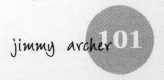

"So, is anything new in Swedesville?" I asked.

"Well, Robertson bought a place next to Jay," my mom said, turning the pages of the brochure.

"Oh, God."

"Yeah. He got let out of prison. I think it's awful, they let him go; s-s-s-sickening what he did."

I looked at my mom in her flowered cotton nightgown, looking to me for the human response of disgust, but I couldn't give it. I was just trying to "boot-up" the incident.

I had started high school two years after it happened, so any news that found its way to me came in drips and clots. I didn't know Jimmy Archer. He'd been immortalized by my high school—as much as a high school could immortalize someone by the occasional retelling of the horrific kidnapping and the small memorial plaque in the main hall. I used to walk by that plaque every day on my way to homeroom. I knew it by heart: THIS PLAQUE IS DEDICATED ON MARCH 16, 1979, TO THE MEMORY OF JIMMY ARCHER 1962–1978. A small metal tag was affixed to the plaque that listed his achievements: Honor Roll, German Club member, Rifle Club member. I had seen pictures of him in class-of-'78 photos. He was thin and pale, with white-blond hair and brown eyes, and he had a small brown mole on his cheek like a speck of dirt in a glass of milk. He was great looking, actually, fragile seeming—but then again I could have been projecting because he was pale and, beyond

quick shots of false hope

that, dead. Students sat in the hall under the Jimmy Archer plaque, they traded homework under it, they forgot about it. But if I were near it at some point in the day, it would strike me how something so bad could happen in a town where nothing ever happens.

"Well," my mom blared, jolting me out of my memory, "your uncle Gene and his partner found him, you know. They knew it was Robertson and the Dove boy that did it—to get ransom money from his dad."

"Yeah, I remember that. Didn't the dad give them the money?"

"Yeah, he did, but by then it was too late. Dove had already left Jimmy in the woods for a few days, tied to a tree. It was Dove who finally told the police where they put 'im. When they got to the tree where they tied Jimmy up, he'd been hit with an ax."

"Oh, Jesus. I thought that wasn't true."

"Yeah, it was true. And those kids were so high on dope, they forgot they did that to him. They cried like hell when they saw it."

"OK, now tell me my other favorite bedtime story."

My mom laughed. "Well, you asked me, didn't you?"

"I guess."

"Hey, this place looks cute," my mom chirped, getting back to the brochure. "You wanna go here for breakfast tomorrow?"

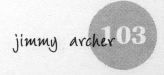

jimmy archer 103

"Yeah," I said without looking. I closed my eyes and thought about Jimmy tied to a tree, as if there could ever be a worse place to wind up when your friends were on dope and swinging axes.

The Customer's Always Right

The headliner concluded his set with a joke about wiping his ass. I can't remember his name now, but he was a nice guy with a lousy act and an anal fixation. Most of the nice guys had lousy anal acts. I guess they had to be nice; it was the least they could do. We were in the banquet room of a hotel chain, which is about as low-grade surreal as it gets. I mean surreal can be laughable—even fun—if you're in a situation that's so absurd that you feel fortunate to be witnessing it. And then there's the banquet-room-on-the-road surreal when you can't stand back and enjoy the strangeness or laugh at it because you're in it and as much a part of it as the tilted letter *K* and the cockeyed letter *Y* that spell the word KOMEDY in the banner over your head.

I was what is known as the "middle act" for the night, which means I'm the act in the middle—not the emcee and/or lamb to slaughter and not the final act whose job it is to leave 'em laughin'.

The master of ceremonies was young and obese. He wore a baggy suit and a bolo tie and cologne as if he were trying to cover up something—a body, perhaps. It was obvious to me that he had studied the hack masters of late-night comedy and was making use of their old impromptu lines like noticing a table of women sitting alone and commenting: "So, where are the men tonight, ladies?"

Invariably, whomever the "hoot" is at the table responds: "We left 'em at home." The audience laughs a little bit. The back-and-forth banter cranks along like a rusty lever on a jack-in-the-box, never really gaining momentum, until finally, as expected, the toy clown pops forth with a joke about the table of women being "lezzies."

After the audience has been thoroughly pandered to, the tired phrase I'm waiting for arrives: "OK, folks, you ready for more show?" He said this as he brought me to the stage with the kind of circus-poodle enthusiasm that makes you smile against your will. (If I had a genuine smile for every one that I've forced—in the presence of one of these guys—I'd be the happiest, most indiscriminate, nonjudgmental sack of benevolence on the planet.)

He read my credits from a 3 x 5 card, which gave a certain amateurish ambience to the lowbrow feel of the evening—especially since I only had two credits.

I walked toward the stage through sixteen rows of ta-

 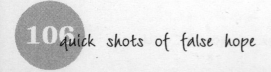
quick shots of false hope

bles and stackable chairs and people turning and clapping, whispering and looking for me.

Whenever I'm in an unfamiliar, potentially hostile, environment—which is almost 88 percent of the time with road gigs—I try to start off with a "Hey we're all friends here, right?" approach and I'm just like you. (Except I stay in crummy hotels, sleep until three, get up and stumble into some anonymous town like a bear looking for food, go back to the hotel, and sit in my own panic scent until it's time to tell jokes to strangers.) I'm your average bear.

As luck would have it, this particular audience decided to enjoy my sense of humor. Before long I found myself breathing comfortably, weaving through topics effortlessly, having the kind of set I didn't think I could have without my home-court advantage. I felt as if I had fallen into a Southwest gully that was going to have me as I was: unformed, unpolished, and unpopular. In fact, their response was so generous, I was letting it erase every bad thing that had happened to me up to that point. They were indulging me, and I held out for more like a pastor awaiting the return of a collection plate. But I also have another theory: Whenever a show feels too good to be true, it's because it is too good to be true.

Just as I had made myself at home on their carpeted stage, about midway through my set, a behemoth of a man and his two barrel-chested dates decided to ruin my good time by requesting that I dance. I'd say a line, there would be a contagious swell of laughter, and when it subsided this hulk of a man would yell, "Dance!" Once he said it, his two lady friends would repeat it. The three of them filled an entire horseshoe-shaped booth with about two hundred and eighty pounds of tattooed pulp apiece.

I had no choice but to launch an attack on the horseshoe booth. I felt confident with the rest of the audience on my side. So I threw a couple of verbal daggers at them. I should probably say darts, since they weren't very sharp, but really, I didn't need much with such easy targets. I asked them if it hurt to get flesh put on their tatoos. The crowd gave me a bit too much credit for that one, but they wanted me to win because of the "I'm-just-like-you" thing. The audience was laughing at everything I said in response to the threesome— they were laughing when I didn't say *anything*. I could just look at my oppressors, and they'd roar. We were working together to flush out the horseshoe booth, and at some point I remember thinking it wasn't fair. When the flesh pit tried to return an insult, their efforts were painfully juvenile and could be handled with a child's na-na-na-na-na. The audience was screaming and feeling delighted with themselves and really didn't need me anymore, so I decided to bid them adieu. I made up names for the hecklers in the horseshoe booth and told them I looked forward to working with them next weekend, and once again the audience applauded and cheered. They cheered for themselves for being among the

quick shots of false hope

winners; they cheered for one woman's victory; they cheered to hear themselves cheering. I glided off the stage, shook the emcee's hand on the steps of the stage, and proudly walked to the exit door without lingering to collect the last accolades of a less-than-honorable triumph.

Smiling to myself, I walked down the hall to the elevator, where I looked at the silver spy mirror in the elevator ceiling and pointed at my reflection, paraphrasing an affirmation: "You are the balls." I walked into my room and locked the door, then I turned on the hot water in the shower and closed the curtain to keep the steam in. Whenever I'm on the road on some shitty hotel-chain gig, I pretend I'm getting a relaxing weekend complete with sleep and sauna—as if I could trick my own mind into thinking we wanted to be there.

Taking off my clothes, I threw them on the floor by the bed. I tucked my hair into a shower cap, walked into my makeshift sauna, eased myself into the tub filled with hot, hot water, and closed my eyes. After about forty minutes I got out of the tub, dried off, dropped my towel on the floor, and walked into the main room with nothing on but the pink shower cap. I peeled down the bedcovers, crawled in, and looked up—only to see the three human boulders I'd destroyed in the banquet room staring at me in complete silence.

"Jesus Christ!" I whispered, like I was telling myself,

"This is bad." I opened my mouth to scream and a squeak came out.

One of the ladies, the one with dark-brown sideburns, cracked, "Where's your big mouth now? Where's your put-downs now, lady?"

"Ahhhhh . . ." I tried to scream again, and this time it was just a faint scratch.

The blond woman who was practically pleasant looking compared to the other two put her open palm to her ear. "What? We didn't hear you, mouth. What did you say?"

She lumbered toward me with her hands out in front of her as if we were about to wrestle. I vaulted out of bed and ran to the bathroom and shut the door behind me, at which point I noticed that there was no lock on the door. I threw myself against the door, remembering that old rule in physics that one person jammed against the door can be an effective wedge against three people, like a lemon wedge is effective in thwarting soda from foaming over the rim of the glass. But the beast turned the knob and came right in; my full body weight had kept her at bay about as well as a wet towel. By this point I was sobbing. I managed to let out an audible scream between sobs as she whisked me out of the bathroom by my hair and threw me onto the bed. If I'd been in a nice hotel, a neighbor might have been concerned by my incessant cries, but at this hotel my slow death sounded like somebody was bein' made love to.

 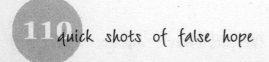
quick shots of false hope

The blond one pinned me on the bed in a matter of seconds. She sat on my stomach and lunked my head against the bedpost by holding a fistful of my hair. The other two were egging her on with cheers of "That's right, Terry! You show 'er, Terry!" Terry let my head drop and grinned at the woman with sideburns, "You know, Candice, this is fun. Do you wanna play with the comedy lady?"

Candice nodded like she was processing official orders from a fellow navy SEAL. She came over and sat on my knees. With the weight of the two women, the bed sank way down in the middle. In pain and becoming dizzy from the bedpost banging, I closed my eyes because I didn't want Terry to be the last thing I saw before I slipped into unconsciousness. I tried to imagine myself leaving my body to rid myself of the intense pain. I wanted my mind to go to a café in Switzerland and hear Mozart's "Utility Vehicle Theme" while my body was being pummeled in Nevada.

"Hey, it ain't time for a nap. Terry, I think you should wake her up."

"Ahh . . ." another raspy, weak cry eked its way out of my body. I kept trying to make noise, hoping that someone would hear me. It was becoming increasingly difficult to breathe, and I began to gasp for air. That's when I felt the first punch. Terry's knuckles came pounding down on my face like a wood beam on a marshmallow. I was crying, and I could feel the bed getting wet under my legs and around the small of my back. My mind wasn't taking me off anywhere; it was sticking around to tell me what was being hit and how hard, like a ring announcer addressing the fans. I couldn't believe that a punch wouldn't knock me out. I was thinking of a movie I'd seen where a woman got punched and was KO'd instantly. It was a black-and-white film, and Cary Grant punched a woman and caught her before she went down. Then he apologized. People knew how to give and take a punch in forties cinema. Punches were so sloppy now, especially for me the way I was hanging on in an uncinematic, unladylike way, my conscious mind blathering on until the punches couldn't land anywhere on my head that could still feel them. It actually seemed like my body had left and my mind was staying, not wanting to miss a thing.

"I'm done," Terry announced. She shook out her hand like it was cramped from making a fist.

"You did a good job, Terr, but I want you to stay put. And, Candy," he instructed, pointing her over to the bed, "you go help her hold down the comedian. I'm gonna take off my pants; show 'er that we still love her."

Terry put her thumb on one side of my face and her four fingers on the other side and pushed in the hollows of my cheeks until the skin pressed hard against my gums; she got off of my stomach and sat back on her knees next to me, still holding my mouth. Just then the bed creaked, and the bedslats at the foot of the bed snapped underneath us, which

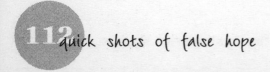

gave the death orgy a downward slant. John was on the bed now. He straddled me with his knees under my arms and leaned forward; with one hand on the headboard and the other on his penis, he stuck himself into my cranked-open mouth.

"OK girls, I think I can handle it now."

Candy and Terry obediently got off of the bed and waddled to the other side of the room.

"I have nothing left," I thought and certainly couldn't salvage any dignity from any of it—being a stand-up, being at this hotel-chain banquet room, dying this way. All I could do was keep it from happening to someone else. I could do it— if I had any strength left. And I did. I bit down hard on John. I felt an immediate, ferocious gush of blood and stringy stuff jettison to the roof of my mouth and all over the back of my throat. I couldn't tell if I was screaming in my mind or actually screaming at that moment in the room. Then I realized that I wasn't screaming at all. I heard the scream again, and I knew it was John. His scream triggered wails from Candice and Terry. I couldn't see anything from where I was, and I couldn't get up. I suddenly had a highly acute sense of different vibrations in the room. I could tell where everyone was and what they were doing from the shaking sounds of their bodies.

I was finally alone on the bed. I was tasting blood and something new and horrible which I assumed was no worse than raw animal entrails—but I've never tried them and never would. In short, the whole mix was making me feel like a volcano ready to puke. And what blasted forth in one violent surge was everything including John's pride and joy.

I felt better knowing it was gone. It seemed inconceivable that no one heard any of it. I was blacking out. "Thank God I'm dead," I thought. "My poor mother is never going to get over this." I couldn't believe I was still conscious enough to hear my own tedious thoughts. "I'm in a hotel room, I had a good set, the money didn't cover my expenses . . ."

My fingers began to tingle. I envisioned myself getting up and putting on a white top hat and looking in the mirror. I adjusted the top hat leaving bloody fingerprints on the rim.

Now, considering it was Tuesday, this pre-show day-dream was only the first of a possible five, since I still had five more days and nights staying at the hotel and performing at their banquet room comedy club "Funny You Should Ask."

quick shots of false hope

Strawberry Swirl

On or around June 10, Tom Arnold called me. My manager had said he and Roseanne had requested my tape, so I wasn't completely stunned. "Hello, Laura, this is Tom Arnold and I'm looking for a wife. Ha-ha, I'm kidding. I've got a wife of course, but I am doing a new TV show and it's something that I think you'd be right for. What I want to do is fly you out here and have a meeting with ya. Get to know you a little bit. Rosie and I saw your act on Comedy Central, and we thought you were real funny."

"Really? Well," I gulped, "thanks."

"Yep," he said. "Rosie and I are big fans of yours."

"Whoa, well, thanks. I really appreciate that."

I flew out to audition for the networks for the part of Tom's wife on his new TV show. I had spoken to a psychic two weeks prior, so I went into the audition with conviction, brass balls, and blind belief because a seer had said it would be so. Another valuable weapon: the confidence that comes from not knowing anything about anything. In fact, I'd say that I won that part by virtue of sailing in there on the gossamer wings of sheer naivete. I went home to Fayetteville to spend some time with relatives I might not get the chance to see once I became a TV star.

My great-aunt June smells like Scotch and Charlie, and if that's not a whiff of blue-collar heaven, then what is? She and my grandmother, her sister, met me at the Buffalo airport. They arrived an hour and a half before my flight was due, which was to be expected. My family celebrated its collective low self-esteem by being grotesquely early for everything. If we had a family crest, it would feature a dragon torching its own ass with fire. Stitched underneath would be our motto: WE'RE NOT GOOD ENOUGH.

On the way home, I asked my grandmother to look for a coffee shop. My grandmother drove cautiously, and by "cautiously" I mean so slowly that there were times when I thought we had stopped to pick someone up. My aunt didn't notice how slowly we were moving because she was preoccupied; she was always thinking about one of two things—herself or Papa. Papa was her boyfriend, Boyd's, nickname. June always called him Papa or Daddy, which repulsed everyone, but we never told her. As we creeped along, June held her ring hand up to the passenger-side window and moved her diamonds around in the sunlight till they pleased her. She put her hand on top of her seat and looked back at me.

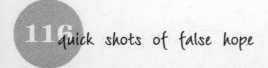 quick shots of false hope

"Papa's real sick, Laura. He's gotta wear a bag."

I knew this wouldn't happen again in my lifetime, so I had to say it. "Wait a minute, June. Are you telling me that Papa's got a brand new bag?"

"Yeah, he ain't never had one a' them before; he's gotta be real careful now of what he eats."

"God, I'm a jerk," I thought.

"He's got a tube coming out of his intestines—it's bright red and, ew, raw lookin', and he's got a clear bag and a rubber band that fits around the tube and the bag. And I had to help him change it, but the nurse cut the holes too big before she give 'em to us, so the bag don't fit right on the tube. So we tried five or six different bags, and Papa's swearin'. Finally we got one to fit on the tube." My aunt sighed and patted the back of her 'do.

"Sooo, now he don't even want to go out 'cuz he's afraid something will happen. I went over to his place the other night, and I serves him some ice cream—you know, that strawberry swirl with real strawberries in and swirl. I go back into the kitchen to fix myself a bowl, and then all a sudden I hear Papa screamin' and I think to myself, What the hell? So I goes back into where Papa's settin', and he's carryin' on. 'Ah, Jesus Christ, June,' he says, 'help me!' It turns out his bag blowed off on account of the strawberry swirl. At first I didn't even see the bag, and I thought, Am I goin' crazy? Course, we had a couple down at the VFW that afternoon, but I thought

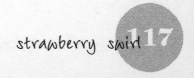

strawberry swirl 117

I had seen it on 'im when I come over with the ice cream. Well, that damn thing had blowed all across the room."

This made my grandma laugh. And then June laughed. "Hey, Sis, it ain't funny, so anyways."

I looked at my grandma's face, and she was really laughing hard now. Her face was beet red, and she was wiping her eyes under her glasses.

My aunt laughed again and tried to hold it back. "Christ, Sis, you wouldn'ta thought it was funny if you was standin' there lookin' at this mess."

Then I started laughing.

"God, yuck! he was all a mess. And I felt bad, you know; Papa was embarrass' about it, but it was just me and God. I've been seein' Papa now for—what is it, Sis? How many years?"

My grandma couldn't answer because she was still laughing so hard, she couldn't stop. I loved seeing my grandma laugh that hard. I looked at her with her tears steaming up her glasses, trying to get herself to stop, and I started laughing again.

"Jeez, Sis, I don't know what kind of pills them doctors give ya for blood pressure, but I'd like to get me some."

Now this made my grandmother choke, and then her laughs came out in long sighs. She pleaded, "Stop making me laugh, June! I can't catch my breath."

"Well"—June looked at me again—"what was I talking about, honey?"

quick shots of false hope

"How long you've known Boyd," I said.

"Sis? How long have I known Boyd?" she asked my grandma again.

"Uhh"—my grandmother was still wiping the tears from under her glasses with her hand—"uh, let's see, you met him after Larry died, and Larry died in May of—oh Christ, I can't think—May of sixty-three; that's right, sixty-three."

"Yeah, so all right, Laura, I know'd Boyd for over . . . let's see, well, for just about thirty years. God, I'm old, ain't I, Sis?"

"Well, you're not as old as me," my grandma said.

My aunt June turned back to me again, and by this time I was leaning forward in an attempt to hold on to the thread of her story.

"So, anyway, what was I—Why don't we stop here, Sis." My aunt pointed at a small diner coming up on the left-hand side of the road.

"All right," my grandma said, and she started to turn in. When we got out of the car, my aunt picked up the story full throttle.

"So, Sis, I was tellin' Laura that Papa was embarrass' about what had happened, but I told him not to be because we know'd each other for so long and I tol' 'im, I said, 'Daddy, we been through worse than this. Like the time I came sick in Las Vegas and I threw up my false teeth into the terlit and we spent the whole night tryin' to fish them damn things out!' "

This started my grandma again. "Quit it, June! You want me to pee my pants before we get in the restaurant?!" My grandma ran in front of us and opened the door. She yelled just inside the doorway at the cashier, "Where are your restrooms, please?"

The cashier pointed to the end of the counter, and my grandma was laughing and running, holding her chest with her arm. My aunt called out to the same cashier, "Can we set anywhere?" The cashier nodded. My aunt and I sat in a booth near the bathrooms.

"Oh, so I told Daddy about the night in Vegas fishin' my teeth out of the terlit 'cuz they went all the way down the hole. We finally got them out around five in the morning. 'Course, we was drinkin'. I can't remember how we did get them out; I think it was with gum and a hanger. So, anyway, Daddy and me was laughin' about that." She sighed and put her ring hand out in front of her on the table, staring at it as if it held the solution to her current dilemma. "It still makes me mad. I mean, it just seems so damn stupid Boyd can't eat ice cream with one a' them on."

My grandma came out of the bathroom.

"You feelin' better, Grandma?" I asked.

"Yeah, it's just June makin' me laugh so."

The waitress brought our menus. June looked for a second and asked, "What you havin', Sis?"

quick shots of false hope

"Oh, I don't know, I haven't even looked yet. Prob'ly a grill' cheese like I always get."

I looked at the two of them looking at their menus.

"Hey, did you guys used to go to parties together? Were you close when you were growing up?"

"No, we fought like hell growing up," June said.

"Yeah, it wasn't till we got a little older, after Dad left, that we started getting along."

"Well, when you were teenagers, did you ever go on double dates or anything?"

"Your grandma and I used to go to the Kinzua Dam together."

"Yep, they was just buildin' it then," my grandma said.

"And that's where we met Johnny and Pitchfork."

"They was cute, too. Pitchfork looked just like Jack Kennedy. He had a problem with his prostate. It went the wrong way. He was always hard."

"Oh, no," I said. "So they called him Pitchfork?"

"Yep. And it went to his head," my grandmother said matter-of-factly. "He ended up at the North Warren asylum 'cuz bein' hard all the time makes you crazy."

"Don't make me crazy," my aunt said, winking. "Ain't that right, Sis?"

Building Dorothy

When I arrived in Los Angeles, I was taken in a town car to the Beverly Holiday Inn. Seeing that I would be staying in a Holiday Inn knocked the wind out of my sails. I thought there had been a mistake. I checked in and dropped my suitcases in the pink seashelled room that looked like one of the dingier rooms I'd stayed in when I was doing stand-up for very little money on the road. I called my manager to complain. How could a star be expected to stay in such a dive? As I was crying to her on the phone a *USA Today* was slipped in under my door. I saw Roseanne's face on the front page and read about how the much-rumored three-way marriage was now in effect. I felt queasy about my career starting on this crummy-hotel ménage-à-trois note. My manager calmed me down. At 10:30 A.M. the following morning I was to meet the cast and take part in what is known as a table read.

We all came in expectantly, pretended to be casual, and snacked at a table full of bagels and fruit. Then we took our name-tagged places at the table. Since I was a lead, I was sitting at the end of the table with Tom. The secondary cast members sat farther away from us, and the audience of writers and executives sat all around us. The reading worked like a charm. The writers, the CBS execs, everyone laughed like hell at everything we said. Even the things that in my opinion were just plain stupid seemed to go over incredibly well. I learned later that it was the writers who'd found our performances so gut busting. Apparently, and understandably so, they laugh really hard at their own jokes to ensure their job security.

We read again on Monday in this same manner but this time for more execs. This time it sucked. Everything I said landed like a nickel thrown down an empty corridor. I tried like mad to juice it up, giving some bits the energy and push that only bad comics on cruise ships have. Still the spinning-nickel feeling. Everything Tom said seemed to get big laughs. Then again, it was clear to me from Audition One that Tom was getting his ass kissed. He could say "Good morning" and the suits would shit themselves laughing. Not me, though. My stunning performance was prompting concern, and on Tuesday, before we were to read on the set, the director asked me in private before we sat down to read our new script if I'd like an acting coach. I was so offended and deflated at that I said: "Wow, was it because the reading was so bad yesterday?"

quick shots of false hope

"No, no," the director assured me, "it's just that you're a comic, and you've never done something like this before, and since you are the lead, they thought it might be helpful."

"Wow," I repeated, still devastated.

"You don't have to, Laura," he said. "They just wanted to give you that option . . . it's totally up to you."

"Oh, it's just an option," I thought to myself. "Like: Do I want toast or a bagel?" I knew it was bad news. Even if I'd wanted an acting coach, I wouldn't have asked. I wouldn't have said, "Well, since you brought me all the way out here, let me shatter your confidence in me by hiring someone to tell me what to do."

I agreed to meet the acting coach. Dag (not short for Dagwood, actually long for inventing a catchy name for oneself) was a heavy man with a beard that someone probably recommended he try as a way to separate his face from his neck. (You've got to draw the line somewhere.) Since I was his yearling, we ate together and took my five-minute breaks together—all so I could take in his words of wisdom. I found out later from a close friend and actor that this coach worked almost exclusively with porn stars trying to break into the other show business. At the time, I didn't know what his track record was; I just figured that if anyone was going to save me, it might as well be him since he was hired to do that. He told me in my dressing room that if I didn't do great he was going to look bad. I should have realized that anyone who cared about looking bad wouldn't have a vanity plate that read STARMKR.

On our first day together, Dag watched the entire run-through and then went over notes with me. He said my body language was shy and uncomfortable, and in the future I should take ballet classes. He said I carried myself like an adolescent girl who had developed too quickly and tried to hide her body.

I thought to myself, "You wish, fatso."

Now I had something to add to my abacus of inadequacy. Not only was my acting questionable, I didn't know how to walk, either. On our lunch break, my acting coach and I went to the commissary and brought our food up to my dressing room so as not to miss a moment of my valuable time. His concern was my "vocal variety." He said that stand-up comics tend to have a delivery that goes against the grain of sitcoms.

"My problem with you is that you're playing one note. Everything is coming out of you like errrrrrrrrrrr."

"Well, that's how I feel," I said.

He laughed. "Well, we still have to work on it. We've got to give you some vocal variety."

Dag suggested that we rehearse Scene E together. In this scene, Tom and I are having a tender, romantic moment, and I'm trying to convince him that I should go back to law school.

quick shots of false hope

TOM (read by Dag): It seemed like our kids were never home. I was starting to get shaky on their names. I missed 'em.

DOROTHY (me): You'll get to spend more time with them while I'm busy with school.

"You're doing *this*, Laura," Dag reprimanded, taking his finger and making a line going down with a sharp incline. "You've got to stay up and then button it."

"Button what?" I asked.

"The word 'school.' It's got to be up. It's gotta be an end. I don't want to feel like you're trailing off into nothing. As an audience member, I want to hear the end of your sentence."

I tried it again.

"Better," he said. "But I still need to see more reaction from you."

"Oh, man, why?" I cried. "I have three sitcom reactions, and I've used them already. You wanna see?" I proceeded to sigh, do a double take, and bug my eyes out in surprise.

"Laura, c'mon," he balked. "I know you're funny, but, look, you've got to go higher and give it energy. We have to build the character of Dorothy. We're taking parts of you, but Dorothy obviously isn't a stand-up comic, right?"

"Yeah," I said, giving up.

"Now, let me ask you: Did Tom or Roseanne give you

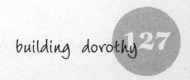

building dorothy 127

any idea of what they were going after in your role? What Dorothy is like?''

''Well, Roseanne said that she saw me as Audrey Meadows,'' I said. ''You know, that I would be like Alice Kramden. That I was smarter than Tom and that I held the house together.''

''Oh, oh, well, that gives me something to work on. Do you have a VCR in your hotel?'' he asked.

''No.''

''OK. Well, would you like to watch some *Honeymooners* episodes at my apartment?''

I went to Dag's place. The first tape he popped in was ''The Champ,'' the episode in which Ralph invites a boxer to live with them. He fast forwarded to Alice's lines then paused the tape at a moment when Alice is standing at the stove. ''Do you see how purposeful she is?'' he asked. ''She knows exactly what she has to do to hurry and fix dinner before Ralph comes home.''

I have to admit, it was thoughtful of Dag to have rented the tapes. He'd even bought me one. He also asked me out. He was giving me too much, really.

The tapes were very helpful. I used a move that Alice used when I turned on the stove. I bent down to look under the pan at the burner to see if it was lit. Actually, I did this about ten times during rehearsal because I really didn't know what else to do around a stove. I had never cooked anything except macaroni and cheese out of the box and Campbell's soup.

The director wanted to keep me "busy" in the kitchen because, one, my lines might come out better if I had a few "activities," and two, a mom with five kids would have a lot of shit to do in the morning.

In the breakfast scene alone, I had over fifteen moves. That's more kitchen moves than I've made in my life so far. I had to: take the juice out of the fridge; fill the kids' glasses; put the juice back in the fridge; pour Tom a cup of coffee; serve everybody their eggs; put on my oven mitt and pull a tray of bacon out of the oven; wait for the boys to spill milk on each other; mop it up; pack their lunches; and remove a brush from my back pocket so I could comb the twins' hair while delivering some pithy line.

I was getting confused about where I was supposed to be, and I wasn't hitting my positions fast enough. At one point I was still fumbling with the twins' lunches, and they had made their entrance to the living room, where I was supposed to be waiting with lunches and brush.

I was so bogged down with my list of physical minutia that when Charlotte, one of my TV twins, said her line, "Mom, will you please tell Emily not to dress like me?" I responded, "Charlotte, you know your mom is nowhere near her mark right now; you'll have to tell her yourself."

A couple of crew members laughed, but I'm sure the

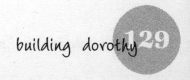

building dorothy 129

director was only thinking about how much I could louse up his camera shots.

Wednesday, after the fourth rehearsal for the network, I saw the head of casting at CBS. I went over to her and thanked her for the acting coach. She hugged me and told me how amazed she was at my progress. On Thursday morning I got up early to eat breakfast with Dag and go over the latest rewrite. We walked to the set together and waited for the table read to begin. Tom wasn't there much, and we did a lot of our morning table reads with the cast and Tom's stand-in. It seemed to me that the stand-in was a stage actor, but too over-the-top for any conventional stage, he was more like an amphitheater actor.

Everyone questioned their own existence after a run-through in front of the execs. Andy, who played the new guy at the roller-coaster factory in our fictional working-class town, sat down at the table last. He asked the director how he thought it had gone the night before. "Not great," he warned. I was thinking that that had been one of my best efforts so far. Anyway, Andy kept pursuing the matter. "So, then, it didn't go well, huh?"

"Andy, does the term 'weak link' mean anything to you?" I called down the table. Everyone laughed. I felt like I belonged.

Tom came in and took the stand-in's seat at the table. This time our performance, like the phoenix from the ashes,

quick shots of false hope

soared to new heights. Clearly beyond the level of "stinky" we had reached the day before. The director even complimented me on my relationship with my son, saying that we had a good rhythm going. "That wasn't all we had going," I thought, remembering how earlier I'd asked my TV son, who was seventeen but playing fourteen, where the pay phone was. He checked me out from top to bottom and replied, "It's outside on your immediate left, babe." "Babe," I grumbled, "I'm your mother for Christ's sake."

As we were blocking another scene, Dag flashed me the A-OK sign, and as we walked to the commissary for lunch he told me I had turned the corner. He said he was going to be with me only until Friday unless I asked to keep him on.

"Yeah," I agreed, "I *definitely* will!" I thought I couldn't do it without him, now that I had turned the corner and everything. In fact, I was depending on Dag so much that I actually looked forward to seeing him every day. For an instant, I wondered if I could go out with someone who had me depending on him so much, but I quickly banished the thought because although I appreciated his guidance, I didn't feel anything for him in that way. At any rate, my boyfriend was supposed to arrive that very day. I'd lost track of the days because my brain was scattered with my two overly choreographed kitchen scenes and my vocal variety.

It was Thursday. As far as I could tell, the table read worked for the director and Tom. The run-through on the set had satisfied my acting coach. Everyone was happy. I sat outside with Dag at the commissary, soaking up some smog.

We went back to the set to rehearse the bedroom scene. We started three times and each time the director added something to complicate the blocking. I felt like a laboratory mouse being given multiple routes to cheese. In this scene I was to slither seductively across the bed and ask Tom to let me go to law school. He misinterprets what I'm asking for and thinks I want another kid. Therein lies the rub!

We went through this scene until the director called for a long break.

I saw Gerri the wardrobe person on the way out, and she ushered me into the trailer to try on some boots. Wardrobe was my favorite part of sitcom life. It was the only place where my opinion counted, and I felt pampered and calm. I hit it off with Gerri and her partner, Pam, straight away. They were genuine: When they smiled, they had nothing to gain. Whenever I saw network people smile, I felt there was a negative sentiment behind it, like: "How the hell did you get here?"

I tried on my boots in the wardrobe trailer, and thanked Gerri and Pam. Gerri was encouraging. "Go work them in, doll, and scuff them up as much as you can!"

It was then that someone knocked on the trailer. It was Lisa, the first AD. "Is Laura there?"

"Yes," I replied.

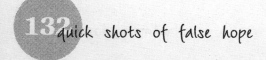 quick shots of false hope

"Laura? Tom and the director want to see you in your dressing room."

I went over to my dressing room and opened the door. Tom, the director, and the head writer were sitting there. The room was a mess, and I resented them for using their own key and waiting for me amidst the shit I hadn't put away. They were all staring at me when I walked in. The mood was not light. I sat down. Tom spoke first.

"Ah, Laura, ah, we think you're not right for this part anymore."

I looked at Tom and saw the head writer to my right peripheral and the director to my left peripheral and put it together that the three of them were there to let me down easy. My first thought was I must not be hearing this correctly. How in the world could three psychics be wrong? I couldn't make eye contact anymore, so I looked down into my address book which I had with me because I was meaning to leave a message at the hotel for my boyfriend, Sean, telling him that I loved him and would be back at 6:30.

"You know, this role has really changed," the director said.

The writer agreed. "Yeah, it really has, Laura; it's . . . we're stressing a more maternal—"

Tom cut him off. "Laura, the thing is, Rosie and I have always surrounded ourselves with experienced actors. Because we know more about being comics than we do about being actors''—he laughed at himself—''and someone's gotta do the acting.''

My head was spinning. How am I going to tell my mother, who already told all of her friends? How can I be such a fucking loser?

''Ya know, Laura, you're a pretty girl,'' the director condescended, killing me with pity. ''You're great to look at. You should take a couple of Meisner . . .''

I didn't look or respond. I thought: ''What if I leapt onto the director and started squeezing his neck with my hands? What would everyone do?''

''Ya know, Laura, one day you'll tell us all to go fuck ourselves,'' he yattered on.

With all of that I still couldn't believe that it was happening. I still needed 100 percent assurance, or maybe I was the only person in the room who hadn't kicked *me* in the balls.

''So, I'm fired!'' I buttoned the word ''fired.''

''I know it seems really awful right now,'' Tom said sincerely, ''but I'm telling you, Laura, we're doing you a favor.''

''Everyone knowing that I got fired from my first acting job is a favor?''

''No. No one's gonna know. If you did the pilot and then got fired, everyone would know.'' He tried to lighten things up. ''Hey, at least you'll get a couple of jokes out of it.''

quick shots of false hope

I was so upset that I didn't know he was kidding, and I said—looking straight at Tom—"Oh, well, then it's all worth it."

I felt the tears catching in my throat, but I didn't sound anything but mad. When Tom said the word "jokes," I immediately thought of going back to a life of stand-up on the road. I felt like I might vomit.

"I was kidding," Tom explained. He prompted the writer, "Dave, you tell her what you told me."

"Laura, honest," Dave dutifully began, "it doesn't have anything to do with you. It just is too much for you to handle. I mean, an actress who's been doing this stuff for ten years would have a hard time doing all the things that you're doing."

"He's right, Laura," the director came in *again*. "If only we had more time and the part wasn't so big. You could do it if it were a smaller part."

"Believe me, Laura," Tom continued, "this seems a lot worse than it is. I know you feel real bad right now—"

"You still get paid for the pilot," the director interjected.

All I could think of was how can I get this firing process over with. I asked some obvious questions.

"Can I get my tickets changed?" I asked.

"Of course," Tom said.

I think my tearless reaction gave him more compassion than he knew he had.

"Laura, what can I do for ya?" he asked.

I shook my head and looked back down at my book. For some reason that was the thing that made me want to cry the most.

"Laura, I'm sorry," Tom said genuinely. "I wanna do something for ya. C'mon, what can I do for ya? Is there something else you want?"

I shook my head and didn't say anything.

"C'mon, Laura, what do you want?" Tom persisted.

"Well," I said, realizing that his guilt might not last forever, "how about giving me a writing job."

"No, Laura, I'm serious," Tom said.

"So am I," I countered.

"Well, all right. Fine. Do you want to write for my show or Roseanne's?" I must've given him an expression like, "Are you kidding?" because he looked at me and laughed.

"Okay, I'm guessing Roseanne's then." Tom clapped his hands once, sealing the deal.

"I'll call your agents and just tell them that you're switching to writing." He gleamed. "We'll just switch your contract." He got up from his chair, and then the director and head writer stood up. "I'll go do that right now," Tom added. Then he paused and turned to me. "Can I get a hug?"

At that moment I thought, "Are these guys just gonna hang out in my dressing room now?" So I hugged him.

"Dave wants a hug, too," Tom said, like a kid asking for a popsicle for his friend.

quick shots of false hope

So I hugged the writer. Then the director came over and looked at me with his arms outstretched, with an expression like, "Whaddya say, you scapegoat good sport?" So of course I had to hug him, too. It seemed implausible. I thought, "Wait, I've got to blow everyone to 'lose' the job?"

When they shut the door, I went into the bathroom, locked the door, and let out a wail of despair that was too good for a lost sitcom part. Pulling myself together, I looked for a pay phone. I called Sean, who had just checked into my room at the hotel minutes before, and started to ask him to pick me up when I began to cry again. I went over to the wardrobe trailer to return my boots and retrieve my sneakers and jacket. Pam was sewing a slip at her table and didn't see my face. She just saw me walk by.

"How are those boots feeling, hon?"

"Well, Pam, God bless ya, it doesn't much matter now. I just got fired."

"You're kidding!" Pam, holding the slip, looked up at me, a stunned look on her face.

"Nope," I said, busying myself with the "activity" of taking off my "mom clothes" to keep from sobbing.

"You're kidding, aren't you Laura?" Pam asked again, even though she must've had a feeling that I wasn't.

"No."

"Oh, God. I'm sorry."

Pam hugged me and I hugged her.

"Well, Laura, we love you."

"Thanks, Pam. Well, I guess it's not terrible. I mean, I'm going to write instead," I said, wishing I hadn't plunged into it with my sad face, wishing I would have taken her condolences and gotten the fuck out of Dodge.

"What?" Pam asked.

"I'm going to write for Roseanne's show. I mean, maybe it's better," I rationalized.

"Great," Pam replied, clearly not understanding. "Have you written before?"

"Yeah, well, I'm a stand-up, and this was my first acting job, so I guess I'm probably more comfortable writing."

"Well, good, so we'll still see you on the lot!"

"Yeah, I think so." I was riding on nothing but the fumes of a stiff-upper-lip attitude.

I walked out of the wardrobe trailer, barely getting out the words "Bye, Pam" before I started sniffling again.

"Bye, sweetie!"

You Always Hurt

At about ten A.M. every morning, all of the writers would wander into the *Roseanne* staff kitchen and get coffee and a bagel, then walk back to the lounge area. Our morning banter would include fabricating gossip about one another like, Pat would say: "Laura, don't you think Steve's a good looking guy? I was driving down Sunset and saw him *paying* for sex." And then Steve would say: "I'm not ashamed, it's not easy to meet women"—then he'd pause—"with penises." We'd laugh and try to top each other with some offensive anecdote about celebrities or death or sleeping with each other, before we were called into the "big room" where eighteen of us converged to be given our writing assignments for the day.

I'd been writing for the *Roseanne* show for eight months when my manager called and asked if I'd like to write for *Saturday Night Live.* "Why?" I asked.

"Well, obviously you don't want to go from writing on a good show to writing on a bad show, but if we could

get you on camera, would you be interested?" she asked in turn.

I thought I'd always regret it if I didn't try, so I flew back to New York to audition at Stand-Up New York with some other female performers. I liked Stand-Up NY despite their unsavory marketing ploys, e.g., a Funniest Chiropractor Contest.

I'd auditioned for *SNL* a couple of times before and not gotten on. Perhaps it was because I thought my chances were so slim that during this audition I had an unusually good set. Either that or the fact that of all the women performing, I was one of the only stand-up comics. The other performers were improv-ers who were darting from one side of the stage to the other, grabbing props like granny glasses and boas and whatever they could use to convey their characters. The audience didn't seem to have the patience for it.

I walked on stage not really caring because I still had a job in L.A. Not feeling desperate must've been my ace in the hole. Everything seemed to work; even the material that only tickles me went over. I had several "applause breaks" during my set and left the stage feeling like I might go kiss myself in the bathroom mirror.

The following Monday I was offered a job on *Saturday Night Live* as a featured player and writer.

I'd been in New York for approximately one week when my friend Linda called me to tell me that my college sweetheart, Joe, had a lump on his neck that might be cancerous.

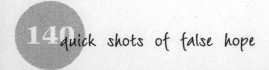

"Linda," I condescended, "you think everything is cancer; it's probably just a cyst. And coming from the person who ran to get a tetanus shot after stepping in a mud puddle, I have to take it with a grain of salt."

"Well, he told me that's what the doctor thought it might be."

"Oh," I reflected. Linda had hypochondriacal tendencies, to say the least, but now I was thinking of a nodule on Joe's neck growing into the proverbial cancer-grapefruit. "Well, has he done anything about it?"

"He's performing with his comedy troupe, The Fun Bags! So, I guess he's not that worried about it." I made a vague plan to go and see The Fun Bags! with Linda even though *SNL* was taking up all of my time. Since I was there when the show was receiving quite possibly the worst press it had ever received, the producers were tweaking everything. We were the latest cast hired to put blood back into the cadaver of sketch comedy. I kept hearing how a "Jane Curtin and Dan Aykroyd-type chemistry" at the Update Desk could rejuvinate the format. And possibly ease the accusations of sexism that were continually streaming in. So, I was all for it when I was asked to audition for the role of coanchor of the Weekend Update segment. I wrote my own update and was put on tape performing it alone and then paired up with a string of *SNL* men: Norm McDonald, Tim Meadows, and Al Franken.

The coanchor auditions were endless. The most torturous part was that I kept hearing that I'd gotten the job. Agents and writers, people I'd never met, would call me to say, "Congratulations!"

"I haven't heard anything," I'd say. "What have you heard?" Of course I would have loved that slot, the most coveted role on the show. Not to mention, an easy transition for a stand-up because it was basically stand-up behind a desk. So every two days or so my agent would call me and say, "It's lookin' good, kiddo. They just have to decide on the guy to put you with." A week or more after I was to officially, definitely know, Lorne called me into his office. I was expecting a landslide of praise; instead he told me that they'd decided to go with one anchor: Norm McDonald.

So, I started my short tenure at SNL with rejection. It was a good thing I got my feet wet so early on. Little did I know I'd soon be set adrift in letdowns.

One night while I was preparing to play Marcia Clark, my steady character on the show, I was sitting in my dressing room with a stocking cap pulled over my pin-curled hair, to make it wig-ready, when I got a call from Linda, telling me that Joe had an aggressive form of cancer called lymphoma and would be starting chemotherapy immediately. I caught a glimpse of myself in the mirror virtually without hair and thought about Joe being sick and petrified and losing his hair. All I knew about chemotherapy was that it didn't always work

quick shots of false hope

and it made you throw up without respite. When I got off the phone with Linda I splashed my face with cold water and took a couple of deep breaths.

Joe sounded good on the phone; he congratulated me on *SNL* and wanted to hear all about it. He told me he was still able to go out and have a beer. In fact, his doctor recommended it.

We arranged to meet at the Westbank Theater on Forty-fourth Street. One of our friends was having a show downstairs, and we agreed to watch it and have a drink. I left the *SNL* offices early on a night when most of the writers stayed until four A.M. and met Joe at the theater entrance. He had lost some patches of hair from chemotherapy and a considerable amount of weight. He looked fucking awful, and I had to pretend that nothing was amiss in his appearance. After the show, which I can barely remember, Joe and I went upstairs to wait for a friend of his that was joining us for drinks. We were laughing and imbibing and, despite the circumstances, were having a good time. When his friend asked me how I dealt with the pressure of being on a live show, I gave a very off-color response, saying I was in danger of becoming a nervous masturbator, like a zoo animal that starts to feel self-conscious in front of spectators. Not only did I fail to impress Joe's friend with my wit, the remark prompted Joe to let out a sigh of disgust. "You're such a pig," he winced. That made me feel so dejected and ugly and crass that I had to leave the table and go cry in the bathroom. I felt ridiculous: Here I was still trying to get Joe's approval with some outrageous statement. Of course, it backfired just as it had when we were going out.

Joe's friend left, and I told Joe how much he had hurt my feelings. I went all the way back to our college and postcollege hurt and made him rummage around in that. "You always make me feel ashamed of myself," I said accusingly. "You just don't respect me," I bulldozed him. "Do you remember that you used to tell me that I didn't know how to put on lipstick?"

I was beyond selfish. I wanted to hurt Joe for not having gotten the lump on his neck checked sooner. The thought of losing him twice was making me crazy and resentful. I was overwrought with feelings, and I couldn't let them out because once I started, there'd be no end. I started crying in front of him and blamed it on being tired. Then we ordered another beer. Joe apologized for calling me a pig. "This cancer thing is making me grouchy," he said. We laughed a little, and he asked me if I ever wore the ring he had given me for college graduation. I stumbled around the answer. "Oh, uh, it's at my mom's house." My response sounded much more like a lie than I'd hoped.

"What did you do with it?" he demanded.

"Oh, God, Joe. I hocked it for an ashtray," I admitted.

"What?!"

"Well, it was actually a nice dish."

quick shots of false hope

"You're kidding me, aren't you?"

"Yesss," I lied.

"You did, didn't you?"

"No," I told him, but I knew that he knew I was lying. "Well, Jesus, Joe, you broke my heart. I didn't want to look at it," I stumbled. "And I was broke. . . ."

"God, I can't believe you," he said.

"I know where it is, I can get it back. The woman who bought it from me still wears it."

"Do you know, I've never given anyone else a ring?" He was so upset and pale and skeletal, it was as if his face was becoming this raw emotion, so worn away by the disease, it was like looking at an exposed nerve. I thought I could throw up from swallowing tears.

"I'll get the ring, Joe," I said with a dry voice.

The next day was a rewrite day at *SNL* and I didn't have to go into the office until two in the afternoon, so I woke up early and went to the pawnshop on Bleecker Street. The old woman who ran the place had the ring on her pinkie. "That's a beautiful ring," I complimented her. "I love garnets."

She cut me off, "It's not for sale."

I contemplated getting into the long history of the ring, but I just didn't have the strength. She'd probably been wearing it for some eight years now. Not to mention, the ring was deeply embedded in her finger like a tree root in a sidewalk.

A few days after our bittersweet reunion, I saw Joe in

the hospital. Shuffling around in the slippers that his mom bought him, rolling his i.v. from the bed to the toilet. There's no more vital Joe, I thought. He looked at my hands.

"You didn't really hock it, did you?"

"No. I don't even know where a pawnshop is," I lied. "I keep it at my mom's to make sure it's safe. And besides, I've got exema all over my hands from the flesh-eating show that is *Saturday Night Live*. I can't even wear rings. I'm going to have my mom send it to me when I get over this stuff."

"Why'd you lie about it?" he wanted to know.

"Well, you called me a pig in front of your friend," I countered.

"He didn't care. He thought you were funny," Joe said.

I changed the subject. "I like your pajamas. Are they fishing lures?" I asked, leaning in to get a closer look at the print.

"Yeah."

"They're hot."

"Will you rub my back?" he asked.

"Yeah."

He rolled onto his side with a frail uncertainty that made me want to fall apart. I sat on the edge of his bed and started to rub his back with my right hand, and then I pressed my fingers into either side of his neck and worked them firmly outward to the end of his shoulders while visualizing myself pressing good health and love into his bony shoulder blades with my palms. We sat like that in silence for a few minutes.

"So," I said, "got any rubbers?"

He laughed.

I made an excuse to leave sooner than I had to, and on the way out I said, "Love ya, Joe. I'll see ya later."

"I love you, too," he called back.

I cried in the elevator and all the way to the curb in front of the hospital, where I hailed a cab. I had to go back to *SNL* to pitch sketch ideas with the rest of the cast to whomever the guest star was that week. For the past month I had been trying to get some of Joe's sketches into the show, having brought his name up to the head writer. I kept telling Joe I would do what I could to get him a job there, which I think gave him something to look forward to even though I warned him I had little clout.

Joe was still writing sketches. I guessed he must've written over a thousand sketches by now, and was so gung-ho about putting shows together and performing that you couldn't help but get sucked into his passion for it. The troupe he started in New York, The Fun Bags!, was gaining quite a reputation. Most of the shows were sold out by the second night. It was actually during The Fun Bags! rehearsals that he'd noticed he had a lump on the side of his neck. He had gone to a specialist, who told him it was benign but that he should get a checkup in a couple of months. The lump kept growing and he went back about six months later; the doctor who told him not to worry referred him to another specialist. The second specialist checked him into the hospital immediately. Joe was going back and forth to the hospital, undergoing tests and giving blood samples, when he got a call from a producer at the *Jon Stewart Show*. Someone in Jon's office had seen The Fun Bags! and wanted Joe to submit his writing samples. He did and got an interview.

I later found out through a friend that Joe's meeting with Jon was unsuccessful. Apparently, Joe talked about ideas and sketches with such full-on enthusiasm and unbridled energy that it was off-putting. Joe was not given the writing job. He continued to work, as he had since arriving in NY five years prior, as a civil servant, processing lawyer's licenses; taking time off to get chemotherapy treatments and, when waking hours permitted, writing sketches for The Fun Bags!

I was staying late at *SNL*, trying to build up an arsenal of funny sketches to pitch for the following week. I'd been told that Roseanne would be hosting. I called her to talk. She said she knew a lot about the history of *SNL* because her manager had been Gilda Radner's and had told her stories about the parties and the blow. "Well, now it's just parties that blow," I replied.

Talking to Roseanne, I got excited about the show again. I was in my office, gulping a stale latte, smoking a cigarette and fiddling with a sketch about a women's prison

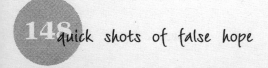

quick shots of false hope

for Roseanne. I was feeling optimistic—either it was actual creative energy or the handful of over-the-counter alertness drugs I'd taken. When Linda called, I wasn't ready to hear what I knew she was going to tell me: Joe had died.

Linda and I took the train to New Haven to attend his funeral. On the train we talked ourselves senseless, and the only rationale we had for Joe's death was this: Life is brutally unfair.

Thank God it was the week after Thanksgiving and that there'd be only one more show before Christmas break. I was trying to get it up for this last show and felt liberated by Roseanne's arrival. Having not seen her since I'd left her show to come to *SNL*, I really looked forward to catching up. And, if she were there, I knew I'd have an ally.

The sketch Roseanne pushed for was "Lock-Up with Bobby Blake," where I played a talk-show host in a women's prison. All the guests were inmates and I introduced Roseanne as "the woman who owns me." Anyway, Lorne and the head writer nixed it. So Roseanne called her manager, and he called Lorne, and the sketch was back in.

I'd used up so much of my already limited drive and concentration to get that sketch in, I felt there was nothing left but the shell of a tired fool. Joe would've sympathized, though; he was under the impression that a sketch on *Saturday Night Live* meant something too.

Lock-Up

I was sitting in my dressing room going over lines and eating my "lucky" hamburger and fries from the deli across the street when my grandmother called. She wanted to know if Roseanne had received the yellow afghan she'd made for her new baby. I don't know why this irritated me. The afghan had been my idea. My grandmother had wanted to give Roseanne something for hiring me to write on her show, and I'd suggested she knit something for Roseanne's baby who was on the way. She made a beautiful white afghan with yellow flowers, which I'd given to one of Roseanne's assistants before the last *Roseanne* taping of the season. I'd written my grandmother's address on the back of the card, flown to New York, and basically forgotten about the gift. I assumed Roseanne had received the blanket and sent my grandmother a thank-you card.

Well, here it was already December, and it dawned on me that maybe Roseanne hadn't gotten the gift. I kept telling my grandma that I would ask Roseanne if she'd gotten the afghan.

My grandmother called me about it twice a day. "Laura, did you ask Roseanne?" she'd want to know.

And I was such an asshole and so involved with myself and learning my all-important prison sketch that I said, "Jesus, Grandma, I'm going to ask her, but she's really busy with sketches and morning sickness."

And then my grandma said, dejectedly, "Well, all right. I'd just like to know because if she didn't get it, then somebody else must have taken it."

"No, I'm sure she got it," I assured her.

"Well, seems strange she hasn't said nothin'."

"Grandma, am I ever gonna hear the end of this?!"

"All right, I'll stop botherin' ya about it," she said. "How's everything else goin'?"

"Good," I replied. "I'll call you later. I love you. Bye." And I hung up the phone. I thought I'd go to the store and get a thank-you card and ask Roseanne to write something on it for my grandmother. That's what I thought I'd do. What I actually did was forget about my grandmother. Instead, I put guests on the list for that night's show and rememorized my lines.

The day of the show, I felt good. I brought one of The Fun Bags! T-shirts to wear during the "goodnights," where everyone waves and gives a fake hug. I also pep talked myself

quick shots of false hope

into performing the shit out of the sketches. I'd do it for Joe. I wanted to instill my performing life with renewed vigor. I had some obstacles. While blocking sketches that afternoon, the director complained, "Laura, can you move to your left? We're still getting you in the shot."

My taking-life-by-the-balls response to that was, "I'm sorry, I keep thinking I'm on this show."

The prison sketch went over well at the eight o'clock dress rehearsal. Afterward we went back to Lorne's office to see what sketches had been chosen. I saw that "Lock-Up with Bobby Blake" was on the board, but it was last. When a sketch is last, that usually means it has a good chance of being cut for time. I felt disappointed but wasn't going to show it. I'd seen grown boys cry in Lorne's office after their sketch was cut, and I'd promised myself to never let any of this shit mean that much.

Not letting the show get to you was nearly impossible. I'd been privy to an exceptionally bleak moment a few shows prior that had let me know, for certain, that I was in the wrong place at the wrong time. Chris and his writing partner, Adam, stopped by the dressing room that Janeane and I shared—probably because it was the most comfortable place to commiserate, and there was always booze. We had all just come upstairs from dress rehearsal and were discussing our least-favorite sketch that week: the Wizard of Oz sketch, a lengthy farce with a switcheroo about what really happened when Dorothy arrived in Oz with her pals. Janeane, still in her Dorothy costume, quite unexpectedly fell on her knees and with her arms outstretched cried, "What have I done? What have I done to my career?!"

In an attempt to spackle over the hole that had just torn open our routine bitch session, Adam snipped, "Uh, this show has never ruined anyone's career."

I looked at Janeane, who seemed to be frozen, arms still pleading to the heavens, and I thought, "Why haven't I pitched a fit? Do I lack the confidence? Or maybe I just get a rush from standing on my knees in front of an audience dressed as a munchkin?" I wouldn't be surprised if I did.

But the night of Roseanne's guest appearance my spirits were high. Even though the sketch I'd written and rewritten with the other writers was scheduled to be last and possibly not on at all, I didn't care; anyway, there wasn't a damn thing I could do about it. The show seemed to be running smoothly without any snags. Finally it was time for my sketch. I heard the intro music and Don Pardo announce, "Live from the Dansmore Correctional Facility, it's Lock-Up with Bobby Blake." I came out center stage in my orange prison jumpsuit to address a small audience of inmates, and as soon as I opened my mouth I saw Lorne by the camera giving me the "wrap it up" or "speed it up" sign with his finger. "Would it be possible to be under more pressure?" I wondered. I raced through the sketch, which was written to look and feel like a

quick shots of false hope

talk show. My sidekick, played by Ellen, was an ornery inmate with a boom box that she'd play at inopportune moments. Rather than agree with everything I said like co-hosts do, her character threatened me every time I tossed off a line to her; I'd comment about some prison-related event and defer to her: "Isn't that right?"

"How 'bout if I come over there and stick you with a knife," she'd sneer. I'd laugh uncomfortably and try to cover in a fake, sunny host-way. Roseanne and Janeane played guests whom I chit-chatted with about what they were doing time for. The sketch garnered gratifying, sustained laughs— and it included dialogue for all of the female cast members— so I considered it a feather in my cap.

After the show, when the cast and crew were leaving to go to the mandatory party, Lorne called out to me in a crowd of people and commented, "Laura, good job tonight."

"Thank you," I gushed. I felt triumphant.

The Kids in the Hall were performing at a theater in the West Village that night, and one of the staff writers, Norm, and I were going to see their show. I was interested in one of them. I was looking forward to it like it was Mardi Gras. During all of this, I'd been struggling to get out of a long relationship with my boyfriend, Sean. Sean knew about the flirtation I'd had with one of the Kids in the Hall members and was upset about it because it happened before our second breakup. We'd officially parted ways, but when he asked me if I was going to their show, I said, "No." I just didn't want to give him another reason to feel slighted.

On Sunday, I was still floating about the sketch the night before. I thought I'd proved myself in some way and that things would be easier at *SNL* from then on. That night, when I was on my way to meet Norm at the Kids in the Hall show, I felt I could finally relax. As I pulled up in the cab, I saw Sean standing on the street.

"Oh, shit!" I said out loud. What did he have to gain by showing up to *catch* me at the Kids in the Hall show? Leaving the cab, I thought it best to get it over with as quickly as possible, so I went over to him.

"Sean?"

"Hey. You should come over here." He motioned me away from the line of people in front of the theater. "I've got something to tell you."

I inched toward him.

"What?" I asked like a bratty child.

"First of all, you lied. And your mom called me looking for you. Your grandma was killed."

"What?"

"C'mon." He brought me over to the pay phone. "You better call your mom."

"Oh, no. What happened? What do you mean killed? Was she murdered?"

"Here, call your mom. Use my calling card."

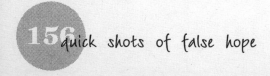

quick shots of false hope

I dialed. "Mom?"

My mom had been crying, which I could hear when she answered the phone with a trying-to-collect-herself voice.

"Laura? I couldn't find you. I didn't know where to call, so I called Sean."

"What happened?

"Grandma was in a car accident."

"She died?"

"Umm-hmm."

"Oh, no! Oh, God! Did somebody hit her?"

"No, she swerved off the road and hit a tree. They said she died instantly."

"Oh, Jesus!"

"Earl's OK. He was with her." Earl was my grandfather, and considering he was my grandmother's third husband, with whom we didn't have much of a relationship, that news wasn't much of a consolation.

"I can't believe it! I can't believe it! Oh, no! I didn't call her back. I . . . she wanted me to just find out if . . . oh, no!" I was sobbing so much, I couldn't talk. "I'll call you when I get home," I managed in short breaths. I walked away from the crowd in front of the theater. Sean helped me into a cab.

Live From P.A.

I was momentarily consoled by a friend who comforted: "Think about the stress you were under in that environment. Where everyone was clawing to be noticed or have something on the show that they'd written." The more I thought about it though, the more ashamed I felt to be one of those guileless under show-biz pressure types.

I packed my clothes to fly home to attend my grandmother's funeral, and I couldn't stop crying. Everything reminded me of her; my closet was filled with clothes that she'd given me while working at the Salvation Army. In fact, the first thing I saw when I opened my top drawer to start packing was a red T-shirt from her with EASILY PERSUADED in silver cursive writing on the front. I decided there was no point in trying to hold back so I cried until my throat was sore.

When I arrived on the predictably cold upstate New York day of December 12, my mother told me that we were greeters at the funeral. This meant that we would have to be at the funeral parlor every day for a certain number of hours.

A few of the "guests," relatives and what-nots, put photos into my grandmother's open casket. One of my distant cousins placed a Christmas present, unwrapped with just a white bow on it, next to her hip. The gift was a mirror with an American Indian painted on it. My mom was standing next to me when this was happening. "You know what this casket needs?" I whispered. "A pharaoh."

My grandmother was in a pine-green lace dress with her hands clasped across her stomach. Cards and cloth-covered boxes lined her body. I was drawn to the Native American woman mirror and leaned forward into my grandmother's casket to get a closer look. The artist titled this "reflective" work: "Navajo Woman At Daybreak." Although, there was no evidence in this painting of time or place. The woman was free-standing, as the painter hadn't given her any ground to stand on. In fact, all she had jutting out from either ear was the line of the horizon and really, isn't that all any of us have?

On the phone that night, I talked to a friend about the painted mirror and how I still had three more days to greet people. "What if there's more shit in her casket tomorrow? What if it gets too heavy to carry?" I wondered.

My friend laughed. "Maybe someone will put a cuckoo clock on her chest! Maybe a dancing Pepsi can!" he suggested.

quick shots of false hope

"Was there anything else besides the painted mirror?" he wanted to know.

"Well, I didn't lift her up or anything, but suffice it to say that I wouldn't be surprised to find a gift certificate for T. J. Maxx in there."

We laughed and kept on making jokes.

Would it have been tacky if I had thrown myself across her coffin and cried, "Why couldn't it have been Aunt Kay? Lord-God, why couldn't it have been Aunt Kay?" I decided I was hopeless. I didn't know how to grieve but I knew I was better at it than the people at my grandmother's funeral who were turning her casket into the Salvation Army drop-off, burying her in her work.

A cousin's cousin or a cousin's son—some kid whom I had never met—knew that I was on *Saturday Night Live* and followed me around the funeral home like a hungry stray. As I was staring into my grandmother's cluttered casket, he announced, "Um, I want to be an actor."

I just laughed, wondering, "Is this really my shitty life right now? Couldn't I sit this out somewhere?"

At the top of Davey Hill, I watched a few of the pallbearers carry the enormous flower arrangement that had been sent from *Saturday Night Live*. I thought it was strange that respects were paid from a TV show and that they had wound up all the way at the end of the road, which was Davey Hill in Youngsville, Pennsylvania. She deserved that much; she had stayed up and watched the show every Saturday night and waited for a punch line or some kind of payoff—like we all did. I never thought it would be this.

I was attending my second funeral in just over two weeks and I could barely comprehend how calamitously wrong everything was. I was half expecting the minister to say: "Yea though I walk through the valley of the shadow of death . . . Live from New York, it's *Saturday Night*." My life had become a ditch flowing with sour milk that I was meant to wade through with bare feet and no end in sight. "Where's the good news?" I wondered. "Where's the bright side to any of this?"

I remembered reading an article about Elizabeth Kubler-Ross's extensive research into coping with death. She had come to the realization that death didn't exist. I thought about her theory and the ugly black suit I'd bought at the mall in Warren, Pennsylvania, and all of the ham that would be choking down tears and vice versa for something that might not exist, "Now that really *is* a waste."

After the funeral we met at a church on Second Street in Youngsville, right near the funeral home, where ham was served by Christians. All I had that week was ham, meat loaf, and Christmas cookies. Earl, my grandmother's third and last husband, who had been in the car with her when she swerved off the road, was sitting next to me at one of the long church-hall tables. My aunt June was sitting across from me, talking

quick shots of false hope

about Earl as if he weren't right next to us. She had a way of saying things under her breath that sounded over her breath. Earl's relatives, who never visited him and about whom my grandma complained constantly, had come in from Chicago to make an empty gesture. Apparently June felt the need to pick up where my grandmother had left off, saying things like, "Well, nice of them to come in and see Earl, now that he hain't got nobody."

Earl was a veteran of the Korean War. He'd had a nervous breakdown while he was there and had to stay in mental institutions from time to time. When he was no longer a "mental patient," he'd stay home with my grandmother and watch televised sports and take pills that made him lethargic. Anyway, Earl and his family were well within earshot when my aunt blurted out: "Well, they gotta take him in tomorrow to see about his testicles, they been hurtin' him so. I mean, Christ, that's the least they can do. They ain't done nothin' for Earl while Rilda was livin'!"

Obviously June was feeling resentful. She wasn't buying into all that after-funeral fellowship crap. I think what was supposed to have happened at this church dinner was a heartfelt communion, a time when friends and family could help one another in dealing with the pain of this loss, a time for ham and every kind of baked casserole and fruited jello. In fact, ham and casserole played such an important role in our lives that my cousin Cheryl mentioned casserole in her eulogy:

"Grandma was just at our house for the family Christmas party, and we all sang songs with Harriet at the piano and then we had some ham and some potato 'n' string-bean casserole, and Grandma said good-bye and that she had to leave before the roads got bad, and we heard a half hour later that she hit a tree."

The after-funeral services get-together was anything but consoling. My aunt Ilene was unable to get herself together emotionally. She traveled with carnival folk—or "carnies"—as a game operator. She's the one who gives fairgoers three balls and encourages them to knock down items that are affixed to the floor. She was my grandmother's forty-three-year-old problem child, and she couldn't keep herself from wailing. This unbridled despair prompted my aunt June, who clearly wanted a fight, to comment, "Well, she should be cryin.' She should be ashamed of herself, the way she misused Mother."

My uncle, who wasn't very smart—or very anything except fat—had a wife who was as simple as she was golden hearted. She apparently needed to feel like she was part of the family; she needed to make a spectacle of herself—which is what any member of my family would do. She was standing in the middle of the two banquet tables as if she were about to make an announcement and started blabbing about a ring on her finger. "Well, you know everybody, uh," she reported across both banquet tables, "this ring is from my future son-in-law!"

quick shots of false hope

I don't know what the hell she expected from that unsolicited tidbit. No one really knew who she was, and they definitely didn't know who her future son-in-law was—and why would he be giving *her* the ring? I think she was expecting applause instead of the ugly Felliniesque stares. Maybe a few laughs? I think she was just trying to be chipper or funny—it was anyone's guess. But after a moment of uncomfortable silence, Aunt June said, "Who cares."

I guess no one had ever told my aunt June to be polite at a time of bereavement.

The Death Dream

I saw a small old woman with brown skin and black hair and deep-set, black soulful eyes. She took my hand, and I willingly followed because I thought she looked very familiar. She was, of course, the Native American woman painted on the mirror in my grandmother's casket. And just like in the painting, we were walking in midair. We walked through nothing for what seemed seconds, and then in the next instant we were standing on the blue-marble floor of a banquet hall. She dropped my hand and stood motionless. I looked at her and then kept walking ahead to a banquet table that didn't end or begin anywhere in sight. I took a plate and stood behind a little girl in a short white-silk dress with a wide green bow tied low on her hips. It seemed like a flapper's dress from the 1920s. The girl turned to look at me and said, "Laura."

And I said, "Oh, Grandma!" and started crying like mad. I fell on my knees to hug her because she was so small. "Grandma, how could you leave me? I miss you so much!"

And she said, "Laura, I'm here."

"No, you're not!" I shouted, sounding much more like a little girl than she did. She put some cookies on my plate, and I walked behind her. I became almost instantly placated by the cookies, and as we walked along the edge of the banquet table, I could see that the entire table was covered with cookies. There were star-shaped cookies with pink sprinkles and chocolate-covered schnauzer-shaped cookies, and every shape, flavor, and color cookie imaginable. I started adding the assortment of cookies to my plate. My grandma turned to me and put her arm around my waist. I looked at her little-girl face, which was so pale and dewy, and her blue-blue eyes that I knew were my grandma's eyes, and I started to cry again.

"Grandma, I'm sorry that I—"

She stopped me. "Oh, I know. Don't worry about it. Why do you always worry about everything, Laura?"

"When am I going to be here, Grandma?" I asked.

"Oh, next year."

"Next year?"

"Oh, no, no. In sixteen birthdays."

"What do you mean, 'birthdays'? Does that mean years?" I asked.

"It's a different language," she replied.

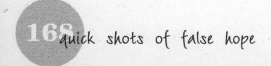

quick shots of false hope

"So, Grandma, I'll be here when I'm forty-six?"

"Yeah, umm-hmm, I think so." She smiled.

"Oh," I said, seemingly pleased with that answer.

Then I woke up.

A Reason For Living

My mom came to visit me in New York about six months after my grandmother's funeral. Mom and Grandma had been very close; they'd shared everything. My mom had depended on her for advice, understanding, and, when I was born, financial support. They both had thought men would make their lives easier, and they were both wrong. I don't think I ever heard my mom or my grandmother complain about their own lot in life; in fact, the only negative aspect of their personalities was their love of bad news. Misfortune was like wine to them. They sniffed the cork of it, poured it for one another, and said, "Thank you, this will be fine." And they weren't particular about how or wherefore the heartache came. It could be an in-law, a cousin, or a family in Tokyo— if it was sad, they'd talk about it for days.

They never started rumors about anyone, but if they had caught wind of anyone's bad luck, it flew out of their mouths at such breakneck speed that no catcher in any baseball club could stop it before it burned a brown hole in your memory forever.

My mom was sitting at my kitchen table, and I poured her a cup of coffee and asked, "So, how's Earl?"

"Well," she said, "he got operated on—you know, for his testicles."

"Uh-huh, I think I read about it in the *Post*," I replied glibly.

"Well, he doesn't seem to be in much pain. And the doctors said he's fine." She took a sip of her coffee. "I think I like instant better," she informed me.

"I don't have instant."

She took another sip. "Oh, this is fine. Ya know, I got my hair done by a girl who used to live downstairs from Earl when he was growin' up. She said Earl's mother used to hit him with a chain."

"Jesus, no!" I begged. "Why? Why would she do that?" I asked, realizing there couldn't be a good reason.

"Well," my mom said thoughtfully, "he was the oldest."

I looked at her for a moment, cherishing her brand of logic. I thought about how much I loved her and how much I wished my grandma were around. And what it would be like if anything was normal.

"Mom, Jesus—so his life has to be sad from start to finish?"

"No," my mom said, "his life ain't so bad. Grandma

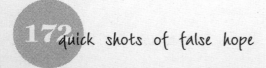

wasn't as mean to him as his mother, and he was with Grandma for over thirty years."

I thought for a second about how much my grandmother yelled at him and that she may not have been the absolute saint that she's become in my memory. I remembered visiting her at home and hearing her scold, "Goddammit, Earl! Sit down and stop following me around!" The drugs had rendered him useless and her redundant.

"She did yell at Earl a lot, though," I said.

"Yeah, but she never hit him."

I laughed. "You're right!" I exclaimed. "Life really is good, isn't it!"